Har

The Ea

Plaque on barn of Leegate Farm
(Leegate Farm –Front Cover)

April 2006   J. Frederick Horridge

No 27 Harwood   J Frederick Horridge
Published by Turton Local History Society
April 2006   ISBN 1-904974-27-9

TURTON LOCAL HISTORY SOCIETY

OFFICERS OF THE SOCIETY

		COMMITTEE MEMBERS
Chairman & Publications	Mrs J Gerrard	Mrs R Anderson
Hon Secretary	Mr P M Harris	Mrs J Bradstock
Hon Treasurer	Mr J F Horridge	Mrs J Francis
Hon Librarian	Mrs J Vickers	Mr J J Francis
		Mrs H Heyes
		Mrs M L Lindop
		Mr C R Walsh

The aim of the Society is to promote an interest in history by discussion, research and record. It is particularly concerned with the history of the old Urban District of Turton, Lancashire and its constituent ancient townships of Bradshaw, Edgworth, Entwistle, Harwood, Longworth, Quarlton and Turton.

This publication is the twenty-seventh issued by the Society; a list of previous publications is given on the inside front cover. In recognition of the years of research undertaken, and as a matter of courtesy and good academic practice, it is expected that due acknowledgement will be made to the author and TLHS when any further use is made of the contents of the publication.

Meetings of the Society are held from September to May inclusive, beginning at 7.30 pm on the third Tuesday of each month at the Barlow Institute, Edgworth. Visitors are welcome.

CONTENTS

ILLUSTRATIONS

AUTHOR'S NOTE

This study stems from the researches over some thirty years of members Jean Vickers and Jim Francis plus the investigations of the writer during the last decade. I am indebted to them both for making available deeds, Wills, plans, photographs, etc, collected from both public and private records and for their advice in the compilation of the publication.

I am grateful for the co-operation of Mr John Calderbank whose papers for the Knott's Estate were collated by Jim Francis and have been particularly useful in resolving the restructuring of Harwood in the 1600s. I also wish to thank Mr Ian Fallows for supplying information on the Hulme Trust and Mr Edward Hardy for contriving the 'artist's impression' of Hardy Cornmill from early documents. Many others too numerous to mention have also contributed information which is much appreciated.

J Frederick Horridge March 2006

Chapter I   HARWOOD TOWNSHIP 1600

At the beginning of the seventeenth century, Harwood was just a small agricultural community of about two hundred and fifty people who lived and worked in the sixteen or so farms and folds spread around the district. The township was one of the seventeen making up the Parish of Bolton-le-Moors (Figure 1) in the County Palatine of Lancashire. and was a provincial member of the Manor of Manchester, not having the distinction of a residential Lordship.

Elizabeth I, the last of the Tudor dynasty, was still Queen of England but was soon to be succeeded by her cousin, James Stuart, the only son of Mary Queen of Scots, who had already been King of Scotland for 36 years since the age of one. He was soon to unite England and Scotland without further conflict, peacefully settle the prolonged war with Spain, and subsequently style himself as 'King of Great Britain'.

Harwood at the time had no town centre as such and the hub of the community would no doubt have been Hardy Cornmill with its central position. Here the farmers would bring their oats, barley or rye to be ground and the townsfolk would gather to exchange the latest news and local gossip, and also buy meal and flour to bake their daily bread.

The township had three areas of common land comprising about a quarter of its total area where the tenants were entitled by their leases to dig turfs, collect reeds, bracken and wood and take sand, gravel, stone and coal for their own use. They were also permitted unlimited grazing for their horses, cattle and sheep.

The layout of the district had evolved over the years with each farmstead having a direct gateway to the commons and the basic thoroughfares forming links between the farms, the cornmill, the local chapels and the church and market at Bolton. These roadways were (and in a few cases still are) rough cart-tracks or bridleways and unfenced in the bounds of the commons. A devised map of Harwood in 1600 with the boundaries of the farms and assumed pattern of thoroughfares at the time is shown in Figure 23.

Rights of way of the thoroughfares were maintained by a Statute of 1325. (R5): *'if any high-wayes or foot-paths to church, mill or market bee stopped or hedged up which have beene accustomed to lye open, you must present (to the court leet) him or them which shut it up, for the King's subjects must not be stopped of his lawful passage to church, mill or market'.* (R2)

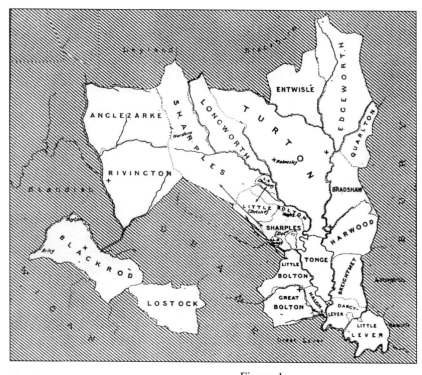

Figure 1
Parish of Bolton-le-Moors c.1900.

Figure 2
*Approximate Borders of the
Ancient Kingdoms c1000.*

There were no local churches during the 1600s and all baptisms, marriages and burials had to be solemnised at the Bolton Parish Church. 'Chapels of ease' had been in existence in the neighbouring townships of Bradshaw and Cockey Moor (Ainsworth) from the early 1500s which some residents would attend to avoid the two or three mile journey to Bolton by horse or on foot.

The Reformation of the English Church in the first half of the 1500s would have had little effect on the everyday lives of the majority of people in the township. The new Book of Common Prayer and the English translation of the Bible would have been introduced into the simplified services of the Anglican Church, but there was much dissent to the new order. The Vicar of Bolton, Ellis Saunderson (see Chapter V) and many of his parishioners were arraigned by the Bishop of Chester on his visitation in 1605 for, amongst other things, not wearing a cassock, performing marriages in private houses, not attending church and not partaking in Holy Communion.

In the same year a small band of the persecuted Catholics in London plotted to blow up the Palace of Westminster on the opening of the first Parliament of James Stuart's reign. If 'Gunpowder Plot' had been successful they would have annihilated the King and Queen along with the assembled Lords and Commons in one blow. The story of the detection of Guy Fawkes lurking in the palace vaults is well recorded and needs no further recount.

The farmhouses and cottages of the period were generally constructed with dry stone external walls, timber framed internal walls and roofed with either thatch or split-stone slates. The cottages would usually have a small garden attached in which the occupants could grow their own fruit and vegetables. Stone for the construction of the buildings and roads was quarried from local delphs. Some coal was being extracted from outcrops in the uplands of the district, but the main domestic fuel would be peat and wood from the commons. The first coal pit recorded in Harwood was in 1620 in the Knotts' uplands.

During the slack seasons, the smaller farmers, workers and their families would have to seek additional employment in other occupations. The most widespread livelihood supplement was the spinning of yarn and weaving of cloth which was carried out in their own homes with chapmen, or agents, supplying the raw materials and marketing the finished goods. Other necessary crafts were undertaken, often on a part-time basis, by individual artisans such as masons, carpenters, thatchers, blacksmiths, wheelwrights, etc.

Names for Harwood featured in the earliest Parish Church registers were Aspinall, Bridge, Brooke, Bromiley, Crompton, Davenport, Entwistle,

Greenhalgh, Hardy, Harrison, Haslam, Haworth, Higson, Holmes, Holt, Horridge, Horrocks, Hough, Isherwood, Knowles, Lomax, Mitchell, Nabbs, Roscoe, Sanderson, Singleton and Tonge. These are the modern spellings for the names which varied considerably in the registers. (R1)

It must be remembered that this was long before the establishment of any formalised spelling and, whilst basic dictionaries were introduced as early as 1604, the English language was only made official for legal documents in 1737. The clergy and merchants were generally literate but only about two thirds of the yeomen and artisans and one fifth of the farm workers could read and write to any degree. This factor is borne out in an Indenture of 1612 (Chapter VI) in which two of the five principle yeomen in the township signed by *'making their mark'*.

The situation was even worse with the womenfolk of whom nine out of ten could not even write their own names and the few existing Wills of the property owning widows are invariably unsigned. However, since the advent of the printing press over a century earlier, some news-sheets and trade notices had started to circulate and literacy was on the increase. (Figure 3)

From the items of clothing bequeathed in some of the early Wills (eg *'my best doublet with silver buttons'*; *'my best boots and spurs'*; *'my yellow stockings'*, etc) one can envisage the homespun 'sunday best' attire of the local people at the time. The men would wear a doublet, shirt, jacket and possibly waistcoat, knee length breeches with hand-knitted stockings and boots, plus for outdoors, a cloak, gloves and hat. The women would wear a petticoat, full length dress or bodice and skirt, often with a pinafore, plus a lined cloak, gloves and gathered hood for outdoors.

The currency in use in the 1600s was primarily the ancient silver penny, a coin of about the same diameter as the present-day penny but thinner. The more recent farthing, halfpenny and silver shilling were in circulation as were the golden noble, sovereign and guinea: pound notes were to come much later. Average earnings per week would be about four shillings for a yeoman and three shillings for an artisan.

Most people, particularly in rural districts such as Harwood, believed in witchcraft, and whilst the practice was widespread in Lancashire during the 1600s, there are no records of any local instances. The only reminder we have today of witchcraft is the old Lancashire custom of displaying horse shoes as a counter-charm.

A
Punctuall Relation of
THE
PASSAGES
IN
LANCASHIRE
this Weeke.

1 *Containing the taking of* Houghton Tower *by the Parliaments Forces, and the perfideous trechery of the Papists who after they had upon Quarter yeelded up the Tower, trecherously set fire to a traine of powder, and blew up Captaine* Starkey *with above a hundred men.*

2 *How the Earle of* Darbies *Forces made an on-set on the Towne of* Boulton, *and was driven off with the losse of a hundred men, and but eight on the Towne side.*

3 *The taking of the Towne and Castle of* Lancaster *by Sergeant ma-jor* Birch.

Printed in the Yeare 1643.

Figure 3 *Printed News-sheet during the Civil War.*

Figure 4
Map of The Manor of Manchester in Salford Hundred c1600.

Figure 5
Natural Features of Turton Urban District.

Chapter II   LOCAL ADMINISTRATION & THE MANORS

In the days of the early Anglo-Saxon Kingdoms the only courts of law and justice were those overlorded by the kings themselves, but as the number of kingdoms reduced and the population increased, this situation became impractical. By the time the kingdoms became unified under Eadred in 946 (Figure 2) most of England had been divided into independant units beginning with the Saxon 'Scirs' in the southeast (Sussex, Kent, Essex etc) and spreading northward with the Mercian Shires (Berkshire, Hertfordshire etc up to Derbyshire and Cheshire). This restructuring was complete south of the Rivers Ribble and Tees before the end of the first millennium AD and by 1300 the boundaries of every county in England had been established more or less as today, if one disregards the local government administrative boundaries introduced post 1974.

Each shire was eventually sub-divided into self-regulating hundreds (bailiwicks, sokes, wapentakes, etc) to maintain law and order and preserve public peace. Ealdermen, Shire Reeves (Sheriffs), Constables and trials by jury were instituted and the Hundred Courts dealt originally with all criminal, civil and ecclesiastical matters. From these humble beginnings sprang the Baron, Leet, Hundred, Shire and Chancery Courts of feudal times and the Magistrates, Coroners, County, Crown and High Courts of recent times.

About thirty years after the Conquest, Albert Grelley (or Greslet), one of the many Norman Barons, was granted a large estate in Salford Hundred ranging from Anglezarke in the northwest to Ashton under Lyne in the southeast.(Figure 4) As the manorial system evolved this major holding developed into the Manor of Manchester held by the Grelley family for eight generations and subsequently containing about fifty townships and hamlets with many regional manors.

During the 1100s, the adjoining townships of Harwood (with Bradshaw) and Turton (with Longworth) had become established on the north eastern border of the manor located within the natural boundaries of the Delph, Eagley, Bradshaw, Quarlton, Roading and Blackshaw Brooks. (Figure 5) The townships were first recorded as *'Harewode and Turton, Lancaster, Salfordshire'* in King John's Great Inquest into land holdings and knights' service of 1212. (R6)

Shortly after the ascendency of Henry II in 1154, Lancashire was instituted as a separate shire held as royal demesne. Two centuries later Henry Grosmont, a fifth generation grandson of Henry II, was invested as the first Duke of Lancaster and at the same time the status of the Shire was raised to that of

County Palatine. (The French 'Conte' was introduced after the Conquest) By 1399 the title had descended via John of Gaunt to Henry Grosmont's grandson, Henry IV and ever since the Dukedom has been held by the sovereign.

There is in existence a register of the Sheriffs of Lancaster continuous from 1156 and for the years of 1602 and 1604 the appointment was held by Sir Edmund Trafford and Sir Nicholas Mosley respectively, both prominent land holders in Harwood at various times as will be noted in the next chapter. Even after more than a thousand years, the High Sheriff is still the Keeper of the Sovereign's Peace in the Shire with wide judicial and administrative duties.

During the 1100s some selected manors and free boroughs were granted the right by the crown to hold local franchise courts to keep the peace and deal with petty criminal offences. A court with this authority was granted to the Manor of Manchester under the mesne Lordship of the Grelleys. This Court Leet as it became known was to continue for seven centuries with much the same area of administration, but diminishing powers, until the institution of the County Court Circuit with the Charter of Incorporation in 1846.

By a Statute of 1325 (R5) the offences *'to be inquired of, presented and punished'* by the Court Leet included *'Affrays and Bloodshed, Sleepers by Day and Walkers by Night, Eavesdroppers, Highways or Footsteps stopped up and Common Bridges broken'*. Also control of *'Tanners, Bakers, Brewers, Assarts, Bounds, Drunkards, Waifs and Strays'* and the provision of *'Stocks and Archery Butts'*. Crimes to be *'only here Inquired of and presented for punishment by the Justices of the Shire'* included petty treason, felonies, embezzlement, rebellion and witchcraft.

In addition to the Court Leet, manorial courts or Court Barons were established in some of the tenanted manors to deal with local estate matters. Typical inquiries at these courts were the improper use of the commons, non-use of the manorial cornmill and maintenance of roads, bridges and water courses. On the death of a tenant, inquiries were made into his service or rental obligations and the succession or assignment of his tenure.

The Court Baron for the township of Manchester, including Harwood, Bradshaw and many other regional manors, was held at the same time and place as the Court Leet and records of the transactions of the two courts are in existence from 1552 until 1846. (R2) The manor of Turton held its own Court Baron for which records exist from 1737 until 1850 during which time the Lordship was held successively by the Chetham, Greene and Kay families. (R7) During the 1600s the Court Leet sat in the Sessions House on the north side of

Market-stead Lane near to its junction with Deans Gate. (Figure 6) The courts were held twice a year within a month of Michaelmas and Easter and generally presided over by the Lord's Steward with a jury of normally thirteen freemen of the Manor. (R8) One of the duties of the court was the appointment of the Borough Reeve, Bailiff, Constables and other more minor officials of the manor. The following presentment of 1654 to the High Constables of the Hundred needs no explanation. (R9)

'Presentments by John Brooke and Henry Ashurst, Cunstables of Harwood as followeth:
Wee present William Hardier and James Isherwood Breadbakers for Harwood and the towne hath mett and thinks them fitt to be continewed. And wee present William Hardier also as Maltster to bee continewed by the consent of the towne. And as for Badgers and Droviers ('licensed' itinerant pedlars) *wee have none within our division. These presentments are made by us afforesaid the 9th of January, 1654 according to a warrant directed to us for that purpose by the High Cunstables.*
By us John Brooke, Henry Ashurst. Cunstables'.

We have no knowledge of any records of the above mentioned township meetings or where they were held at the time. A later petition from the inhabitants of Harwood to the Justices of the Peace suggests that the diligence of the Constable was not quite as it should have been. (Figure 7)

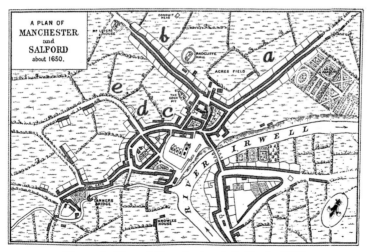

Figure 6 *Map of Manchester & Salford c1650.*
(a) Deans Gate (b) Market-stead Lane
(c) Hanging Ditch (d) Withingreave (e) Shude Hill

9

To the right worshipfull the Justices of the Peace att their Sessions of Peace houlden att Manchester the 16th day of April, 1657.

The humble petition of the inhabitants of Harwood in the Parish of Boulton sheweth. That whereas John Brooke of Harwood aforesaid husbandman hathe served for the office of Constable within the said Towne for the space of three years last past and hathe received severall sommes of money assessed and collected within the said Towne and hathe not given anie account thereof to your petitioner and that there is neither rogue's posts, stocks nor buts within the said Township accordinge as by the Statute is required.

May it therefore please your good worships that the said John Brooke may be ordered by this Courte to make his account to your petitioner and likewise that your worships would be pleased to grant your order that a certaine somme of money may be assessed and collected within the said Township for the making of the rogue's post, stocks and buts and such other necessaries as are awaiting in the said Towne and your petitioners will ever pray etc.

(Clerk of the Peace note: To account to and present Court to raise a sum of money to build stockes. To send this to Thomas Russell aforesaid.)'

Thirty years later the inhabitants of Harwood again complained to the Justices of the Peace about payment for repairs to the access road across Nab Moor.

To their Majesties Justices of the Peace and Quorum at the Quarter Sessions at Manchester the 25th day of July, 1690.

(A *Quorum* originally denoted certain learned Justices of the Peace whose presence was necessary to constitute a bench).

The humble petition of the Inhabitants of the Hamlett of Harwood in the Parish of Boulton, Humbly sheweth:

That your petitioners hath paid for the straites upon default of the Causey over Nabb Moore and the Lanes adjoyning hereunto lying in Harwood aforesaid not being repaired in tyme the sums £5.16s.4d which charge lyes almost wholly upon the aforesaid Hamlett.

And your petitioners further sheweth that they have laid out in repairing of the said Lanes upon their own charge the sum of 19 Pounds since the said Causey of Nabb Moore was finished.

Therefore your petitioners humbly pray you order of this Court to be granted to impower Will Hilton Esq and Jas Chetham Esq two of their said Majesties Justices of the Peace and Quorum to inspect the overseers account and to order the overplus of the moneys (if any there be) to be paid to the aforesaid inhabitants of the Hamlett of Harwood. And your petitioners will ever pray etc.

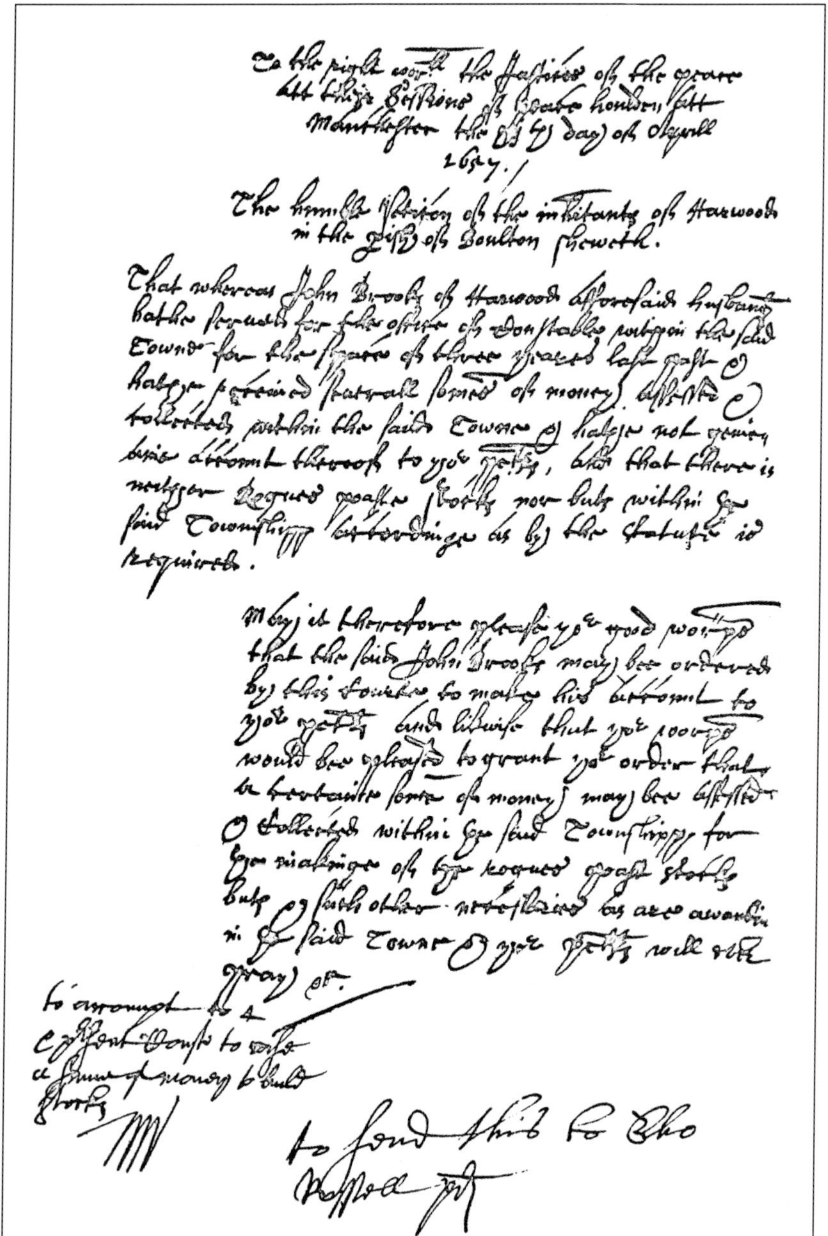

Figure 7 *Petition to the Justices of the Peace 1657.*

The people of Harwood must have been quite law abiding as very few items concerning incidents in the township are noted in the surviving records of the courts. One entry in the Constables Accounts for Michaelmas, 1616 reads: *'13th Marche. Item paide for Whippinge Elizabeth Romesden of Harwoodd for Filchinge. 4d'*. (R2) Most of the items refer to the appointment of jurymen and Richard Aspinall, Giles Aynesworth, Edward Brooke, John Brooke, Edward Greenhalgh, John Greenhalgh, Robert Haslame, Raufe Higson and James Isherwood, all *'gentlemen of Harwood'* and freemen of the manor (R8) were recorded as jurors at various Inquisitions between 1615 and 1639.

As mentioned earlier in the chapter, 'crimes' of witchcraft had to be dealt with by the *'Justices of the Shire'* and the most notable case ever in the county was in August 1612 when nineteen suspects from Samlesbury and the Forest of Pendle districts were tried at Lancaster Castle. After a hearing of only two days, ten of the accused were found guilty and publicly hung the following day. The clerk for the trial, Thomas Potts, was instructed to write a detailed report of the proceedings and in 1613 he published *'The Wonderful Discoverie of Witches in the Countie of Lancaster'*. In 1849 this account was taken up and romanticised by Harrison Ainsworth, the Manchester historical novelist in his classic *'The Lancashire Witches'*. Witchcraft was prevalent in Britain over roughly three centuries but the 1600s saw the greatest activity.

The Grelleys' Lordship of the Manor of Manchester ended in 1309 when Thomas, a bachelor and the eighth Lord, formally granted the Manor to Sir John la Warre, the husband of his only sister Joan. The la Warre family then held the Manor until 1426 when on the death of Thomas la Warre, again a bachelor, it passed to Sir Reginald West, the brother-in-law of his widowed sister Joan. The Lordship was maintained by the West family for 150 years until by deeds of 1579/81 it was transferred from Thomas West to John Lacey of London for £3000. In 1596, Nicholas Mosley purchased the Manor from his friend John Lacey for £3500 which the family then held for ten generations until 1846 when the manorial rights were sold to the newly formed Corporation of Manchester for £200,000.

In 1600 not one of the inhabitants of Harwood was a freeholder and every acre of land in the district was in the possession of families residing elsewhere. This situation was soon to change however but before considering the impending reorganisation let us first review who held the land at that time and how it was acquired. To concur with documents of the period, all references to land areas in the following pages will be defined in Cheshire Measure which was customary in South Lancashire until the late 1800s. The Cheshire Acre measures a little more than double the Statute Acre. (R10)

Chapter III LAND HOLDINGS BEFORE 1600

Soon after the Norman Conquest, William I decreed that only the crown could own land and this factor has been the basis of English land law ever since. He granted about half the land in the kingdom to some 180 Great Barons (tenants-in-chief) and the remainder was divided between the religious houses and the royal estates.

The barons and church held their tenures (feuds) in return for services to the sovereign, which could be of a military, personal or religious nature and in order to fulfil these service obligations the tenants-in-chief subgranted (infeudated) portions of their estates to lesser tenants.

The second cousin of William I, Roger de Poitou was granted the land *'betwixt Ribble and Mersey'* which later became the southern half of Lancashire. After a rebellion of Roger and his brothers in 1102 his estates were confiscated by Henry I and his former subinfeudatories became themselves tenants-in-chief, holding their estates directly of the crown.

In 1086, Albert Grelley held land in Blackburn Hundred but by the time of Roger's eviction he had been subgranted the large manor of Manchester in Salford Hundred which he then held directly of the monarch. The Grelleys' manor house was positioned on the east side of the River Irwell on an 'island' surrounded by the converging River Irk and the man-made Hanging Ditch. (later the site of Chetham's School) Their watermill was located nearby on the River Irk in Mill Gate. (Figure 6)

The manor of Salford to the west of the River Irwell had been retained by Roger de Poitou but with King Henry's requisition this became royal estate and the two manors were thus separated and remain so to this day.

Albert Grelley's crown mesnes consisted of 45,500 acres for the service of $5\frac{1}{2}$ knights and extended over half of the total area of Salford Hundred. He also held large estates in Suffolk, Lincolnshire, Nottinghamshire and Norfolk for a further $6\frac{1}{2}$ knights' service. (R11) The twelve feudal knights of Robert Grelley II, the great great grandson of Albert, are recorded as accompanying Richard I to Normandy c1195.

In 1212, Harwood (including Bradshaw) was recorded as being held jointly by Alexander de Harwood and Roger de Samlesbury (R6) under a tenure of one sixth of a knight's service from the above Robert Grelley. The total area of the joint township was 1132 acres of which 156 acres in the southern half of the district were maintained as common land.

The process of subinfeudation of land from tenant to tenant with each being responsible to their superior for certain services was prohibited by a statute of 1290. (*Quia Emptores*) Thereafter each tenant *'held of the chief lord of that fee'* (the tenant-in-chief) who held directly of the crown.

Even before 1290 however, feudal tenures by knights' service were on the wane and as early as 1243 Droylsden and Failsworth are recorded as having *'changed to socage tenure'* ('plough service' - later changed to annual rent).

It would appear that the part tenancy held by Alexander de Harwood in 1212 formed the northern half of the township which in the late 1200s was acquired by the Bradshaw family possibly by purchase from Alan de Harwood. A branch of the ancient Bradshaw family had long been established in the upper part of Harwood which had adopted their name. It is documented that Henry Bradshaw held land in Harwood in 1235 and in 1306 Robert Bradshaw was noted as a free tenant of Bradshaw held of Robert Grelley. (R12)

The other joint tenant of the township, Roger de Samlesbury, had three granddaughters by his son William and wife Davina of whom Margery, the eldest died without issue. The other two daughters who shared the inheritance were Cecily who married John d'Ewias and Elizabeth who married Robert de Holland.

Earlier in the 1200s a large holding in Harwood had somehow been acquired by the Trafford family and when Sir Henry de Trafford succeeded his father in 1291 he inherited the title to land in Harwood which he defended in a suit of the following year. By 1302 it was documented that Henry de Trafford, Robert de Holland and John d'Ewias jointly held one eighth of a knight's fee in Harwood from Thomas Grelley. He was the last of the Grelley Lords and the fee would seem to be the last reference to feudal military services recorded in Harwood.

The portion held by John d'Ewias and wife Cecily descended by the marriage of their granddaughter to Sir Gilbert Southworth whose family are recorded as early as 1212 in land transactions with the Ainsworth family. The Southworths retained their holding until 1506 when John Southworth lost possession and the estate was eventually acquired by the Ainsworths, initially with Thomas and later with Robert and Giles.

The portion held by Robert de Holland and wife Elizabeth descended down the male line of the family until it was forfeited after the Battle of Bosworth in 1485 and granted, along with many other estates, to Sir William Stanley for his crucial role in the conflict.

The Trafford family retained their holdings in the centre of Harwood over nine generations until 1589 when they sold it in a large parcel including land in Barton and Edgworth to Nicholas Mosley. The conveyance was by Final Concord and a copy of the original counterparts of the agreement held by the Mosleys is shown in Figure 8.

Final Concords (R13) were fictitious court actions and a common device at the time for breaking an entail of restrictive descent on a tenure. An abridged translation of the Mosley-Trafford Agreement of 1589 is presented below. The numbers, acreages and consideration of £300 cited would be false figures.

> *'This is the final concord made in the Court ... before John Clenche ... and Thomas Walmysley ... between Nicholas Mossely citizen and clothmaker of London, plaintiff and Edmund Trafford, Knight and Edmund Trafford, Esquire, son and heir apparent of the said Edmund, deforciants concerning thirty two messuages, thirty two tofts, one water mill, thirty two gardens, three hundred acres of land, one hundred acres of meadow, three hundred acres of pasture, one thousand acres of moor, one thousand acres of heath and heather, and one thousand acres of moss land with appurtenances in Edgworth, Harwood and Barton whereupon a plea of covenant was summoned between them in the same court ... of the gift of the said Edmund Trafford, Knight and the said Edmund Trafford, Esquire ... to the said Nicholas and his heirs against all men forever ... for three hundred pounds sterling.* Lancaster*

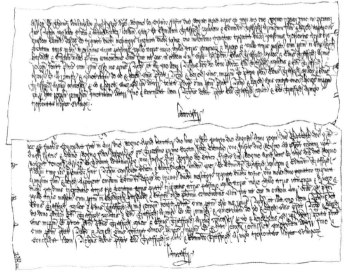

Figure 8
Final Concord Mosley-Trafford, 4th August 1589.

15

The established land holdings in Harwood at 1600 are shown in Fig 23. To recapitulate, the Stanleys held 48 acres in the south western corner with Crook Fold, and the Ainsworths held the eastern area of 82 acres with Aspmah Fold and Isherwood Fold. The Mosleys held the main part of 300 acres including Longworths Farm, Knotts Farms, the two Brookfold Farms, Greenhalgh Fold, Hoyles Fold, Hill Farm, Heights Farm, Davenport Fold, Lee Gate Farm, Dewhursts Farm, Lomax Fold and Hardy Cornmill. These three principal tenants also held proportional areas of the 156 acres of common land subject to the estate rights and interests of the commoners.

In 1694 an *'inquiry of the encroachments and inclosures'* of the commons was undertaken and the findings of the enquiry are presented in full in Appendix A7. With the steady increase in population, the area of the commons was gradually eroded by encroachment around the edges to build farm buildings and dwellings and by the time of the Harwood Enclosures of 1797 (R3) the overall area had been reduced from 156 to 143 acres. The above enclosures would seemingly account for a large part of this discrepancy of 13 acres. The report conveniently records the names of about fifty tenants of Harwood at the end of the 17th century.

The enquiry was undertaken and signed by the three *Pinners for the Common*, namely Richard Lomax, George Haslam and Michael Mutchill. The pinners (or pinders) were appointed by the township to round up stray cattle and sheep and impound them in the *pinfold* which was a small enclosure located at the southerly tip of Little Harwood Lee. (Figure 23) The outline of the pinfold can still be seen opposite the White Horse Inn on Stitch mi Lane.

Before considering the Harwood tenancy changes of the 1600s, the administration of the Monarchy, the State and the Church will now be examined to see how legislation and events at the time would affect the lives of the local people.

An abnormality of the period worth mention was the retention of the old Julian Calendar in Britain which was ten days (eleven after 1700) behind the Gregorian Calendar adopted in Western Europe in 1582. This variance was eventually rectified by the omission of eleven days in September 1752 but the term included in that year's taxes, tithes or rents was thus marginally reduced. These charges were normally settled on March 25th (Lady Day) and to correct the deficit the Board of Stamps and Taxes duly extended their financial year to end on April 5th where it remains to this day. Also in 1752 the start of the Civil or Legal year was moved from Lady Day to January 1st (New Year's Day) and consequently earlier documents drawn up between these days were dated the previous year. After four centuries or so these variations are mainly of theoretical interest and all dates in the following text are as recorded in the relevant documents.

Chapter IV THE STUARTS, THE CIVIL WAR & THE RESTORATION

At the time Charles Stuart ascended to the throne in 1625, Parliament was composed of two Houses as today. The House of Lords met at the Palace of Westminster and consisted of the peers of the realm along with the lawlords and the major bishops. The House of Commons met next door at the converted Chapel of St Stephen and the assembly had since 1295 included two members from each county, generally the principal landed gentry, merchants, lawyers, etc, and two burgesses from each city and borough. For Lancashire these constituencies were Lancaster, Liverpool, Preston, Wigan, Clitheroe and Newton but parliamentary representation in the county was spasmodic with only occasional returns.

Charles' reign was very controversial with irregular parliaments and harsh, unfair taxes, and over the years, his relationship with Parliament deteriorated. In 1640, when he recalled Parliament after ruling alone for eleven years, the new Parliament endeavoured to establish a balanced constitution with power shared by the King, the Lords and the Commons. In an attempt to foster political support for their cause they issued a Protestation in May of 1641. All Englishmen of eighteen and over were required to take the oath and the 84 signatories for Harwood are listed in Appendix A1. It is estimated that these 84 males would represent about a quarter of the population of the township making the total population in 1641 to be around 350. The Protestation Oath is presented below:

I, A. B. doe, in the Presence of Almightie God, promise, vow, and protest to maintaine and defend, so farre as lawfullie I may with my Life Power, and Estate, the true Reformed Protestant Religion expressed in the Doctrine of the Church of England against all Poperie and Popish Innovations, within this Realme contrarie to the same Doctrine and according to the Dutie of my Allegiance to His Magesties Royall Person, Honor and Estate.

As also the Power and Privileges of Parliament, the Lawfull Rights and Liberties of the subject, and every Person that maketh this Protestation in whatsoever hee shall doe in the lawfull pursuence of the same. And to my power and as faire as lawfullie I may, I will oppose, and by all good waies and meanes endeavor to bring to condigne Punishment all such as shall, either by Force, practice, Counsells, Plotts, Conspiracies, or otherwise do anie thing to the contrary of anie thing in this present Protestation contained. And further, that I shall in all just and honorable waies endeaver to preserve the Union and Peace betwixt the three Kingdomes of England, Scotland and Ireland. And neither for Hope, Feare nor other Respect Relinquish this Promise, Vow and Protestation.

The power struggle between King and Parliament eventually combined with a religious division in the country between the Anglican Church who supported the Royalists and the Puritans who sided with the Parliamentarians. Things came to a head in November 1641 when Parliament demanded a replacement of the King's Ministers. Charles responded with an attempt to arrest five Members of the Commons which misfired and he immediately withdrew from Westminster. In August 1642 he raised the 'royal standard' at Nottingham and the civil war began.

Local hostilities broke out at Manchester the following month with an attack by Royalist infantry and cavalry led by James Stanley, but after almost a week of skirmishes and negotiations, the Royalists gave up and retreated. During this campaign James Stanley (Lord Strange) succeeded to the title of Seventh Earl of Derby on his father's death. Whilst Lancashire, particularly Salford Hundred, was a stronghold of Puritanism and Parliamentarianism, no major battles took place in the county.

In the following year Bolton was attacked on two occasions; the first on the 16th February, 1643 was by the local militia from Wigan; the second attack six weeks later on the 28th March was led by the Earl of Derby but both attacks were unsuccessful with only a few casualties.

In February 1644, whilst the Earl of Derby was dealing with troubles in the Isle of Man, his moated mansion at Lathom came under seige from the Parliamentarians and his indomitable wife, Charlotte de Tremoile, after conducting the defence of the house for ten weeks, appealed for help to her 'relative', Prince Rupert. (Charlotte's cousin, William II of Orange had recently married Rupert's cousin Mary, the King's eldest daughter). On May 25th, 1644 Prince Rupert with about 10,000 men crossed the Mersey on route to relieve Lathom House and the Parliamentary blockade of some 2500 men under Colonel Alexander Rigby thus abandoned Lathom to take refuge in Bolton, arriving there about midnight on May 27th. The Royalists accordingly re-routed to Bolton and on approaching the town from the southwest the following day, they halted about noon on Dean Moor for a council of war. (Figure 9)

From their viewpoint (near Plodder Lane) some 250ft above the town they planned an attack. There was very little to be seen on the intervening moorland apart from a few farmsteads on Lever Edge between Barden Brook and Lever Brook. The town was protected naturally on the northern border by the River Croal (Bolton River) and on the southern side by a clay and mud wall about 6ft thick which had been built on the edge of the commons near the present location of Great Moor Street. The first attack by Prince Rupert's force in the afternoon of May 28th failed after half an hour's hard fighting with the loss of around 200 men.

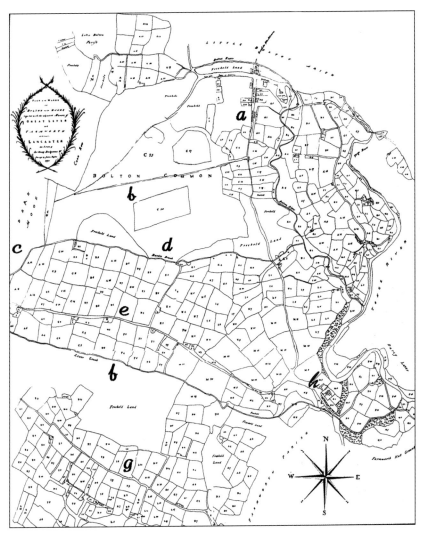

Figure 9 *Plan of Bolton in the Moors together with the adjacent Moors of
Great Lever and Farnworth in the county of Lancaster.
The estate of Sir Henry Bridgeman Bt.
Surveyed by James Byden 1770
(a) Bradshawgate (b) Great Moor Street
(c) Dean Moor (d) Barden Brook
(e) Lever Edge (f) Lever Brook
(g) Plodder Lane (h) Great Lever Hall.*

19

A second attack the next morning led by the Earl of Derby had more success and they managed to breach the defensive wall and enter the town at Private Acres. (later New Acres then Acresfield) The Royalist troops rushed in and brutal fighting followed with the carnage and plundering continuing in the fields and townships for many miles around. The loss of life in the massacre was estimated at the time to be about a thousand in the town plus some 250 of the attacking soldiers, but these figures are now considered to be somewhat overstated.

Prince Rupert stayed in Bolton until 31st May to refresh his troops before setting them on a two day march to his next objective, Liverpool. The 'Bolton Massacre' had been the first Royalist success after several defeats but the dreadful incident has been described as the most infamous of the Civil War.

Colonel Rigby with his shattered troops retreated eastward in the direction of Bradford and may possibly have rested overnight at a fold in Stitch mi Lane on their way to Cockey Moor. This farmstead, later named Goodwin Fold, (see Greenhalgh Fold, Chapter VIII) had been established about 1630 by James Crompton, a notable parliamentarian and puritan from Breightmet Fold. Several pieces of armour, sabres and a quantity of lead shot were found at the farm during demolition of an old wall in 1830.

The '78 of Bolton slayne the 28th of May 1644' entered in the burial registers of the Bolton Parish Church suggests a much lower number of casualties than the original estimates, but it is thought that many victims were buried privately. The registers of 1644 show no noticeable increase in the average number of burials of people from Harwood with only eight interments recorded in the year of which half were infants.

The Civil War ended with the surrender of Charles I shortly after the siege of Oxford by Oliver Cromwell's New Model Army in the spring of 1646. An unstable period of government followed with the disgruntled Army and multisected Church demanding radical constitutional and ecclesiastical reforms. This led to the formation of the partisan 'Rump Parliament' in 1648 and the trial and execution of Charles I the following year.

To conduct the eight day trial of the king a republican provincial judge, John Bradshaw (Figure 10) was appointed President of the High Court of Justice. He belonged to the Bradshaw family of Marple, Cheshire who in 1693 purchased the estates in Bradshaw from the local branch of the ancient family. As president of the court, John Bradshaw was the first to sign the death warrant of Charles I with Oliver Cromwell following as the third signatory. (FIgure 11)

Figure 10
John Bradshaw
President of the High
Court of Justice in 1649.

Figure 11 *Death Warrant of Charles I 1649.*
Note John Bradshaw and Oliver Cromwell as 1st and 3rd signatories.

In August, 1651 the Earl of Derby, shortly after his return from the Isle of Man, surrendered to the Parliamentarians at Nantwich and was imprisoned in Chester Castle. There he was court martialled on a charge of high treason and beheaded at Bolton two months later. No doubt some Harwood people would have been at the Market Cross for the public execution of the Earl, which was allegedly carried out by an Edgworth farmer named George Whowell whose family had been savaged by the Royalists.

The Commonwealth period with republican rule succeeded the regicide to be supplanted in 1653 by the personal rule of Oliver Cromwell under the Protectorate. After Cromwell's death in 1658 there followed two years of unstable government by an interim Parliament which led to the restoration of the monarchy and two months after the reinstatement of Charles II in 1660, twenty-nine of the signatories of his father's death warrant were put on trial for regicide, ten of whom were sentenced to death. The trial was presided over by Sir Orlando Bridgeman, the Chief Justice of the Common Pleas whose father, John Bridgeman, the Bishop of Chester, had purchased the manor of Great Lever in 1629 from the Ashton family, successors to the Levers. A fifth generation grandson of Bishop Bridgeman, Sir Henry, was created Baron Bradford (of Shropshire) in 1794 and a survey of his Great Lever estates and Manorial Hall are shown in Figure 9.

Charles II had inherited an impoverished Exchequer and found it necessary to impose a series of taxes to pay for the Dutch and French Wars. The first tax was a form of Capital Levy based on the number of hearths in a household. Payment was two shillings per annum for each hearth in houses worth more than twenty shillings per year. Householders being assessed as unable to pay were exempt from the tax. Records of Hearth Taxes were lodged from 1662 to 1666 and 1669 to 1674 inclusive but those of March 1664 are the most complete with the names of the householders and the number of hearths. The returns of the 1664 Hearth Tax for Harwood are presented in Appendix A2. The owners of two hearths would probably be yeomen or artisans.

The second imposition was the Poll Tax based on the number of heads (or polls) in a household. This form of tax had been granted by 'parliament' as far back as 1377 but it proved very unpopular and was discontinued. It was revived with intermittent Poll Taxes after the Restoration but few detailed returns of these survive. A list of Harwood residents who paid a Poll Tax in 1678 is presented in Appendix A3. The levy was one shilling per head for both men and women over the age of sixteen plus two shillings per servant. People considered too poor by the assessors Thomas Davenport and Richard Masson were exempt from payment.

Chapter V THE CHURCH

In late Saxon times when the land between the Ribble and Mersey was the most northerly part of Mercia (Figure 2) the ecclesiastical centre for the whole of the ancient kingdom was the Diocese of Lichfield in Staffordshire. The Court of the Diocese dealt mainly with appointments of the clergy, collection of tithes, administration of Wills and estate matters. By the time of the Conquest the ancient kingdoms had become obsolete but Lichfield remained the ecclesiastical authority of South Lancashire until the Reformation when the Diocese was transferred by Henry VIII to Chester in 1544.

The nearest church to Harwood recorded in the Domesday Book was *'the church of St Mary in Mamecestre'* which was located in Acres Field to the east of Deans Gate. (the present site of St Anns Church - Figure 6) This modest timber church was abandoned in 1215 and a new stone church built by Robert Grelley II on the site of the present Cathedral within the fortified confines of his Manor House.

How and when the ancient Parish of Bolton-le-Moors (Figure 1) was established is unknown but there is evidence of a Saxon chapel formerly on the site of the Parish Church. The foundation of a Bolton prebend and vicarage are recorded at Lichfield in 1253 and the succession of the clergy of Bolton is registered back to that time. A new Parish Church of St Peter was built c1420 (Figure 54) and a Grammar School founded a century later in 1524. As mentioned in Chapter I, 'chapels of ease' were established in the early 1500s in the adjacent townships of Bradshaw in the Parish of Bolton and Cockey Moor in the Parish of Middleton.

The registration of baptisms, marriages and burials for the Parish of Bolton commenced 1573 and baptisms were conducted at Bradshaw Chapel for a short period after the Restoration. A 'Parochial Survey of Lancashire' of 1650 (R16) advocated the formation of a separate parish for Bradshaw Chapel to include the whole of Harwood and part of Turton but it was two centuries before the division transpired as will be noted in Chapter IX.

Wills involving the disposal of land and/or property became part of the title to the estate. They were required to be proved at the Ecclesiastical Court, but in general they were administered locally by either the Warden of the Collegiate Church of Manchester or the Vicar of Bolton, surrogates to the Bishop of Chester. In the Protectorate period (1653-1660) bishoprics and ecclesiastical courts were discontinued as were the titles archbishop, bishop and dean. During this period no Wills were lodged at Chester (see Appendix A4) and the Prerogative Court of Canterbury, in the form of a civil Court of Probate of Wills, was the only court.

Personal property was dealt with in the Testament and before 1785 it was obligatory to provide an inventory of the effects of the deceased compiled by two non-beneficiary parties. Widows and single women were allowed to make Wills but with married women, all the property was considered to belong to the husband.

Local Church Wardens were elected and for Harwood in the 1600s included John and George Brooke, Thomas Davenport, John Crompton, Richard Greenhalgh, Ellis Hardy, Richard and Robert Haslam, Richard Haworth, James Heaton and Richard and John Lomax. In 1724 the Church Wardens of Bolton ordered a new hearse for the parish, and the following memorandum should be self-explanatory:

> 'November 5th, 1724. Memorandum:
> It is then agreed betwixt Mr Henry Eskrick and the rest of the Church Wardens and Ralph Greenhaulgh of Harwood, wheelwright. That the said Ralph Greenhaulgh shall be obliged to make an Herse of oakwood japaned with black for the use of the Parish of Bolton in form and manner as follows: Impris: That the said Ralph Greenhaulgh shall be obliged to make the wheels five foot an half, strakes or tier full two inches, four frets of a naith, (hub) bushes, axle-tree and all other instruments fitting for the Herse and Wheels (Harness being excepted) and all the foresaiid matters at the price of seven pounds and ten shllings, to be finished in the space of three months in which said agreement we have set our hands.
> Henry Eskrick Ralph Greenhaulgh
> Also 'tis agreed that a Death's Head and two Cross Bones on the door behind is to be drawn'.

To pay for the upkeep of the church, tithes were introduced about the eighth century and followed old Jewish law which contended that one tenth of the produce of the land should be forfeited for the provision of spiritual services. Originally the tithes were settled in produce which was stored in barns similar to the one at Bradshaw Hall Fold (rebuilt in 1999) which was thought to have been a 'tithe barn'. The settlements were later commuted to 'corn rents' based on the current price of corn.

In 1305 the Township of Harwood paid a tithe to the Dean and Chapter of Lichfield in the form of a rental: 'The tythe of Harwood set to Roger o'th' Wood for vijs'. (7 shillings) The tithe rate for the township had almost quadrupled by 1650 when the 'Parochial Survey of Lancashire' (R20) recorded: 'There is payed by the Inhabitants of Harwood by way of prescription the some of twentysix shillings & eight pence for tyth corn worth six pounds per annum' . The tithe was to be paid to the Dean and Chapter of Chester via 'John Bradshawe Esquier', who was apparently acting as a local collecting agent.

24

Payments by the householders of Harwood in 1650 were *'Every howse one penny, every garden one penny, one or more henns one halfpenny, if they have any ground one penny, every cowe and calfe one penny or one halfpenny, every sheepe with wooll on his backe one halfpenny, every farrow cowe one penny, every fole one penny, every swarme of bees one penny.'* Annual payments would have averaged about eight pence per household. The tithe system survived both the Conquest and Reformation of the Church virtually unchanged. Settlements 'in kind' were discontinued with the Tithe Commutation Act of 1836 and the tithe for Harwood was finally discharged by the Tithe Commissioners in 1854 for a lump sum of £80 representing twenty four annual payments. (A5)

Before 1532, the clergy were required to pay a tenth of their annual income to Rome but with the Annates Act of Henry VIII this revenue was diverted to the Crown. A typical annual payment in 1624 was £1.16s paid to the Exchequer by Mr William Greg, the Vicar of Bolton. (denoting an annual income of £18) These monies were held by the Exchequer and formed the basis of the Queen Anne's Bounty founded in 1702 to support the Church of England clergy.

Following the Reformation, a section of the clergy who preferred a 'pure' religion without the surviving ceremonies of the Roman Catholic Church chose 'not to conform' to the rituals of the Anglican Church. This was the origin of the Puritan movement which developed into the various nonconformist and dissenting groups of the 1600s.

A notable local nonconformist was the Rev Richard Goodwin whose name is retained in Goodwin Fold, Stitch mi Lane as noted in Chapter VIII. He was born in Sussex, graduated at Emmanuel College, Cambridge and in 1641 was ordained by Bishop Bridgeman at Great Lever Hall. (Figure 12) His first benefice was at Cockey Chapel but towards the end of the Civil War he took refuge at Hull and later London. He returned to Bolton in 1647 as assistant to the Parish Priest, John Harpur on whose death in 1657 he was appointed Vicar of Bolton.

In an attempt to entrench Anglicanism after the Restoration, the 1662 Act of Uniformity was introduced compelling all clergy to conform to the Articles of the Church of England and to use the Book of Common Prayer. Richard Goodwin was one of the 2000 ministers who refused, and he and eight other clerics from the Bolton district were ejected from their offices. Two more statutes were enacted to further suppress nonconformity. The Conventicle Act of 1664 restricted private religious meetings to five persons and the Five Mile Act of 1665 forbade dissenting clergy from coming within five miles of their former parishes. These Acts seriously restricted the preaching activities of Richard Goodwin who moved into Manchester to study chemistry but after the

Act of Indulgence in 1672 which allowed dissenting ministers to again conduct services without persecution, Richard Goodwin was granted a license to preach.

He formed the first nonconformist meeting house in Bolton on the corner of Bradshawgate and Mealhouse Lane (now HSBC Bank) where he preached until his death at the age of 73. He was buried within Bolton Parish Church on Xmas Day 1685, his wife Mary having predeceased him by 35 years. The congregation of the meeting house later transferred to Bank Street Chapel when this was built in 1696.

Richard's comprehensive Will, self-written the year before he died, named ten beneficiaries of which the last, his nephew James Okey, was to receive *'all my lande in Harewood with all the appartananances therof'* plus the residue of his estate provided he changed his name to James Goodwin (as well as James Okey). There were two other provisos: Meal worth £20 to £30 bought at a favourable price should be stocked and sold to the poor at below market price when opportune: £5 yearly to be bestowed in 10s shares to needy or sick diligent families. *(no common beggars)*

In an Indenture of 1729 the above endowment of Richard Goodwin was combined with a bequest of Samuel Brookes to form the Goodwin and Brooke's Charity. Sums of £100 and £400 were settled with Arthur Bromiley and Thomas Davenport, the church warden and overseer to the poor of Harwood respectively who, along with the trustees of the charity, were to distribute the accrued interest to the poor at their discretion. It is not known if James Okey ever changed his surname to Goodwin.

Figure 12
Great Lever Hall Acquired by Bishop John Bridgeman in 1629 and held for six generations. Demolished 1972.

Chapter VI THE FIVE YEOMEN

The Mosleys originated in Moseley near Wolverhampton and in the 1400s a branch of the family established themselves at Hough End, Chorlton-cum-Hardy. During the next century Nicholas Mosley and his brother Anthony amassed great wealth as woollen merchants operating between Manchester and London. In 1595 Nicholas was knighted after serving as Lord Mayor of London and the following year, as noted in Chapter II, he bought the Manorial Rights of Manchester from his friend John Lacey for £3500.

After the decline of feudalism many yeomen farmers had gained an important position in local society and started to purchase the properties in their possession. This would appear to have been the situation in Harwood which led to an unusual sale of the total holdings of the Mosley family in the township. By an Indenture dated May 1st, 1612, Sir Nicholas Mosley and his son, Edward, the Attorney General of the Duchy of Lancaster, conveyed *'in consideration of eleven hundred pounds ... the manor or Lordship of Harwood with all ... messuages, mylles, tofts, crofts, cottages, lands, tenements, meadows, lesowes & pastures, commons, waste, woods, etc'*, to a partnership of five yeomen of Harwood.

This partnership, namely Matthew Harrison, Henry Haworth, Raufe Higson, Lawrence Horrocks and Edward Greenhalgh, was entrusted to convey the various tenements located in their 300 acre holding to the tenants in possession, including themselves. The tenants were to pay *'a rateable and proportional part of the purchase money if so minded'* for acquisition of *'certain messuages and lands in the hands of occupiers ... their heirs and assigns shall at all times hereafter have hold and peaceably and quietly enjoye the said messuage or tenement, land, etc'*.

To summarise the above agreement, the leases to the occupiers were to be freehold and the proportional payments were apparently to be in ratio to the acreage of land held. They would hold a proportional part of the common land conveyed to the five yeoman subject to the *'estate rights and interests in to upon and out of the said waste grounds'* of the commoners and be allotted a proportional part of the commons if at any time they were *'enclosed'*. (ie legally partitioned and awarded to the principal land-holders - R3) They had *'rights of common'* which included *'common of pasture'* at all times for all manner of cattle and also *'common of turbary'* to dig and carry away turfs, stone, slate, clay, marle, etc. If by general consent any *'pittes for getting stones, slates and coles'* were to be dug in the commons, any profits would be proportioned amongst the leaseholders.

The trusteeship of five yeomen commenced the conveyancing of the various properties to the occupants eighteen months after their acquisition from the Mosleys and the transactions over the next few years are scheduled in Figure 13. The details of the first five conveyances listed have been obtained from existing deeds of which brief extracts follow.

LONGWORTHS FARM
Indenture of October 6th, 1613. The five yeomen conveyed to Henry Ashurst of Asheton (assignee for John Entwistle) *'a part of Harwood to John Entwistle of Entwistle for the sum of £113 being a rateable portion of the total sum of £1100'*. Witnessed by Raufe Higson, Henry Haworth, Edward Greenhalghe, Lawrence Horrocks & Mathewe Haryson

(Lancashire Record Office Ref QDD 21/20)

KNOTTS FARM (East & West)
Indenture of December 21st, 1613. Four of the five yeomen conveyed to the fifth yeoman, Henry Haworth *'for the sum of one hundred and three score pounds, being a proportional part of the said sum...messuage, howses, orchards, meadows, pastures, etc...in his tenure or occupation'*. Witnessed by Raufe Higson, Edward Greenhalghe, Lawrence Horrocks & Mathewe Haryson. (the latter two witnesses made their mark)

(Knotts Estate Papers. Mr John Calderbank)

BROOKFOLD (North)
Indenture of August 8th, 1615. The five yeomen conveyed to Giles Aynesworth of Aynesworth for a consideration of £38 *'certain messuages and lands in the hands of occupiers named and a thirty-fifth part of the moors, commons, etc, belonging to the manor of Harwood'*. Witnessed by Edward Bromiley, Edmund Brooke & John Brooke (Chethams Library. Hulme Deed 108)

BROOKFOLD (South)
Indenture of January 1st 1616. The five yeomen conveyed an occupancy to *'John, son and heir of William Brooke of Harwood, yeoman, for a consideration of two and thirty pounds'*. Witnessed by William Horrocks, Thomas Bromiley, John Crompton, Thomas Walch & Ellis Hardier.

(Chethams Library. Hulme Deed 109)

GREENHALGH FOLD
Indenture of August 20th, 1617. Four of the five yeomen conveyed *'for the sum of three score and fourteen pounds ...being a proportionable part of the sum of eleven hundred pounds...in performance of the said trust...to the said Edward Greenhalgh...that messuage or tenement...and also the eighteenth part of the wastes and commons'*. Witnessed by Raufe Higson, Henry Haworth, Lawrence Horrocks & Mathewe Haryson.   (Bolton Libraries. Archives Ref ZZ/52/1)

Property	Acres	Cost	Occupier	Indenture
Longworths	31	£113	John Entwistle?	Oct 6th 1613
*Knotts (East & West)	44	£160	Henry Haworth	Dec 21st 1613
Brookfold (North)	11	£38	Giles Ainsworth	Aug 8th 1615
Brookfold (South)	9	£32	John Brooke	Jan 1st 1616
*Greenhalgh Fold	20	£74	Edward Greenhalgh	Aug 20th 1617
*Hoyles Fold	21	£78?	Matthew Harrison	
*Heights	31	£113?	Raufe Higson?	
*Hill	25	£92?	Lawrence Horrocks	
Lee Gate	27	£100?	Arthur Bromiley	
Dewhursts	42	£156?	Thomas Bromiley	
Davenport Fold	8	£30?	John Davenport	
Lomax Fold	18	£66?	John Lomax	
Hardy Mill	13	£48?	Wylliam Hardy	
Totals	300	£1100	($£3^2/_3$ per acre)	

Figure 13 *Schedule of Conveyances 1613 to c1620.*
Tenancies of the Five Yeomen indicated *

Of the remaining conveyances, whilst no deeds are available, the identity of the tenants is generally indicated in other documents. The scheduled acreages have been measured from the available plans and the assessed costs are based on these acreages.

The *freehold* leases purchased by the occupiers would be 'for ever' without any stipulated end date and the estate could be disposed of without restriction. Conveyances were by *Livery of Seisin*, which involved handing over part of the property (ie a turf) for an entry fee (*quit rent*) in the presence of witnesses. For safe remembrance the conveyances were normally recorded with an *Indenture of Feoffment*. This was a deed written twice (or more) on a single piece of parchment which was separated with indented (wavy) cuts and a part retained by each party. (A deed involving one party only had a straight or polled edge and was called a *Deed Poll*). Inheritance of the property would normally be to the heir apparent but if the descent was restricted to a particular person, the lease was said to be *entailed* and could not be sold.

Previous to the above restructuring the occupants had held their tenancies direct from the land-holders generally by *leasehold* for a limited number of years or lives. A lease granted for a specified period such as 99 or 999 years could be conditionally transferred to another person for the residue of the specified period. A lease granted for several lives (usually three relatives of the lessee) was almost equivalent to a freehold in that it had no definite end date. Normally the lease was allowed to continue until the death of the last surviving party and regranted with the inclusion of another nominated person.

Of these early tenancies it is known that Peter Greenhalgh held land from Edmund Trafford in 1523, John Bradshaw held land in the Riding Gate area valued at 3s 4d per annum from Sir Edmund Trafford in 1548, Edmund Brooke held the leasehold of Brookfold North for 80 years at 6s.8d per annum from Sir Nicholas Mosley in 1607 and Elizabeth Haslam held Top o'th' Knotts Farm (East) from Sir Nicholas Mosley in 1607.

Besides *freehold and leasehold*, a third form of estate lease in use at the time, but not applicable in the Manor of Manchester, was *copyhold* which was for property held by customary tenants of a manor. Title to the property was entered on the manor court rolls with a 'copy held' by the tenant. With these leases the tenant was not protected by common law and they were finally abolished by an Act of 1922 when existing *copyholds* were converted into *freeholds*. The only known local copyhold leases were in the neighbouring Manor of Tottington where the court rolls from 1504 to 1587 (R14) record numerous inquisitions into the registration and surrender of these leases by the customary tenants.

Chapter VII   THE STANLEY AND AINSWORTH HOLDINGS

The family of Stanley has been described as one of the most illustrious in the whole range of the British peerage and for over a thousand years has been *'distinguished and promoted by royal favour to the highest posts of honour and trust'*. Before the Conquest, the Stanleys held large estates at Stonely in Staffordshire from where their family name originated. During the 1300s they acquired by marriage the houses of Lathom and Knowsley in Lancashire and for services in the conflict at Bramham Moor in 1406 they were granted the Isle of Man which they ruled until 1736. The Earldom of Derby (R15) was conferred upon Sir Thomas Stanley by Henry VII in 1485 after the Battle of Bosworth and as mentioned in Chapter III, he was granted the land in Harwood at the same time.

The Harwood holding of some 48 acres contained only one farmstead in the 1600s which later became known as Crook Fold. Over the years two other farms, Shore and Alders, were established in the southern half of the estate and these developments will be examined in the next chapter. The Stanley family eventually sold all their estate and interest in the cottages and land adjoining Crooks c1885.

The Ainsworth family of Ainsworth date back to the 1100s and Thomas Ainsworth and his wife Joan were holding land and property in Breightmet and Harwood in 1542. When Thomas died in 1594 he left to Robert Ainsworth, the son of his brother Peter, fourteen messuages and a water mill. By 1600 the whole Ainsworth family estate was evidently in the possession of Giles Ainsworth with the 82 acres of land in Harwood being shared by the two tenancies of Aspmah Fold and Isherwood Fold. Another branch of the Ainsworth family settled in Smithills and during the 1700s developed the large bleaching concern in the area. (R17).

Giles Ainsworth and his wife Sicely had two daughters, Jane who married Richard Meadowcroft from Breightmet and Katherine who married Richard Banastre also from Breightmet. The latter couple lived at Oakenbottom and after the death of Giles in 1621 they acquired the whole Ainsworth estate by Final Concords of 1623, 1632 and 1635. Richard and Katherine Banastre had two daughters of whom the eldest, Christian, married William Hulme in 1630. William owned estates in Reddish and Prestwich and lived at Withingreave Hall (later Withy Grove) on Shude Hill, Manchester. (Figure 6) Three years after their marriage, Christian died leaving an only son, William, and four years later William senior also died. His estates were left in trust with his brother John until William junior reached the age of twenty-one.

The younger daughter of the Banastres, Katherine, married Alexander Baguley from Oakenbottom in 1642 and they had four sons, Richard, William, Alexander and Christopher. Later, as the only surviving daughter of the Banastres, Katherine with her husband Alexander inherited the whole of the Ainsworth estates on the death of her father in 1652.

William Hulme Junior, being left an orphan in 1637 at the tender age of six, appears to have been brought up at Oakenbottom by his aunt Katherine with her four children. When he was seventeen he matriculated at Brasenose College, Oxford and in 1650 was admitted to Grays Inn but never called to the bar. Three years later he married Elizabeth, daughter of Ralph Robinson of Kearsley Hall (Figure 14) where the couple then lived until William's death. They had an only son named Banastre who died in 1673 at the age of seventeen after a playground fight at Manchester Grammar School. On reaching the age of twenty-one in 1652, William Hulme inherited extensive estates mainly in Lancashire and Cheshire and three years later he purchased the whole Ainsworth estate from his aunt and uncle, Katherine and Alexander Baguley. He later acquired other farms in the Harwood area. (see Brookfold Farms)

When William Hulme 'of Kearsley' died in 1691, after making generous provision for his wife he bequeathed some of his estates (including those in Harwood) to an endowment fund to support 'four of the poor sort of batchellors of arts after such degree taken in Brazen-nose Colledge in Oxford' to continue their education for a further four years. When Elizabeth Hulme died nine years later, having no heir, the remainder of the estate passed to the recently formed Hulme Trust. (R18)

Figure 14
Kearsley Hall
The home of
William Hulme
and his wife
Elizabeth from
1653 to 1691.

Chapter VIII   THE FARMSTEADS, FOLDS AND CORNMILL

Whilst the original thatched, timbered and dry-stone walled farmhouses have long since disappeared, at the time of writing some form of buildings still exist on the majority of farms considered in this chapter. All but four of these properties are illustrated in the following pages.

After acquiring the freehold leases, the farmers and their descendants began to build more substantial buildings, generally with external walls in random or coursed stonework and many with inner walls of timber framing and wattle and daub infill, or in some cases, riven oak planks. Two surviving examples of this form of construction are Brookfold Farm (North) and Hill Farm. (Figures 19 & 31)

The history of all the original farms and folds (fold meaning here a farmstead surrounded by a cluster of cottages) are examined generally for the period 1600 to 1800 with brief summaries of any later subtenanted farms. As the population of the township increased over the two centuries numerous other minor properties were established, many as pre-enclosure encroachments. These include homesteads (tofts), dwelling houses (messuages), industrial premises and small holdings such as the Nook, Old Pit, Folly Farm, Bottoms and Walk Mill but only the major tenancies have been considered in this overall study.

The areas quoted for the various estates are denoted in Cheshire Measure as before and, having been assessed from ancient maps, deed plans, land tax returns, etc, are not presented as exact acreages.

(A) LONGWORTHS (Figure 15) (A1) Longsight Farm (Figure 16)

This farm in the extreme west of the township would appear to have been the first of the occupancies to be conveyed by the five yeomen. From a deed of October 1613 it would seem that John Entwistle of Entwistle and his assignee, Henry Ashurst of Asheton, purchased the freehold of the 31 acre farm in the tenure of Roger Haslome for £113.

Within a few years 23 acres of the land to the north of the estate were developed into Longsight Farm and occupied by Lawrence and John Crompton of the Harwood branch of that extensive family.

After Roger Haslome died in 1651, the remaining 8 acres to the south of the estate were purchased by James Longworth who occupied the farmhouse with his wife Margery and sons James and John. Son James succeeded to the farm after his widowed mother died in 1686 and in 1694 he was recorded as having encroached onto the commons with *'two little buildings'*. (A7) When he died in

Figure 15 *Longworths Farm c1950.*
Occupied by three generations of the Longworth family from c1660.

Figure 16 *The remains of Longsight Farm 1959.*
The farm was purchased by Robert Lever in 1637 as an
endowment to Bolton School and later came to be known as School Farm.

1728 James left eight children but had previously sold the freehold of the farm (which had acquired their name) for £310 to his eldest son John. By the time of the Enclosures of Harwood in 1797, Edmund Heaton was registered as the freeholder of Longworths.

Returning to the larger Longsight Farm, this was purchased in 1637 by Robert Lever, a bachelor and cotton merchant from London along with his brothers John and William, the objective being to make an endowment to some educational or religious undertaking. When Robert died in 1644, the property was left in trust with his brothers who both died shortly afterwards and the farm then descended to William's son, William Lever of Kersal.

The Bolton Grammar School was refounded in 1657 with income from Longsight Farm plus other monies bequeathed by Robert Lever and two years later the farm was conveyed by his nephew William to the executors of the school for five shillings with a peppercorn rent of sixpence per annum. In 1757 Robert Walch was granted a tenancy of the farm for life at a rent of £20 per year and the Walch family then occupied it until the mid 1800s. The Governors of Bolton School held the freehold of the farm in the Enclosures of 1797.

James Hardcastle from Bradshaw Bleachworks bought the water rights of the land in 1838 for £800. School farm, as it had come to be known, along with Clegg's Cottage at Bottom o'th' Moor were sold by the Governors of Bolton School to the Starkie family in 1895 for £2600; the Starkies had owned the Walk Mill (or Fulling Mill) and smallholding adjacent to Bradshaw Brook for many centuries.

(B) KNOTTS (East & West) (Figures 17 & 18)

This farmstead known collectively as Top o'th' Knotts (R19) is located in the northern uplands of Harwood and consists of two individual farms of 20 and 24 acres. (East & West have been adopted for clarification)

In the late 1500s William Haslam occupied the east farm with his wife Elizabeth and young son Robert. William died in 1603 and four years later Elizabeth released the farm from Sir Nicholas Mosley. Soon afterwards she remarried, her second husband being her neighbour, Henry Haworth from the west farm who was one of the five yeomen trustees. In 1613 he purchased the freeholds of both farms from his four colleagues for £160. The following year his newly adopted stepson, Robert Haslam then aged eighteen, married Marie Astley from Turton. A marriage settlement was agreed in 1620 whereby the bride's father was to pay Henry Haworth £120 and in turn the estate was to devolve to Robert Haslam.

Figure 17 *Top o'th' Knotts (East). Front view from south.*
Occupied by William Haslam in the late 1500s.
His widow, Elizabeth, married her neighbour Henry Haworth in 1607.

Figure 18 *Top o'th' Knotts (West). Front view from north.*
Henry Haworth purchased both East and West farms in 1613.
The family of his heir, Robert Haslam, retained the West farm until 1894.

Henry and Elizabeth were to remain in occupancy of west farm rent free for life but regrettably they both died within two years.

In 1630 Robert Haslam split the estate by selling the east farm to William Crompton of Breightmet for £160 but he had retained part of the property and nine years later, along with his son William and William Crompton, he sold the farm to Ralph Platt of Rumworth for £270. The Platt family then held the east farm until 1660 when the freehold was purchased for £360 by Thomas Lever with his son Nathan of Chamber Hall, Bolton

The Haslams retained and occupied the west farm from 1630 until 1894. The nine succeeding generations of the family worked the farm and also a coal extraction operation starting from a small pit to the north of the estate first recorded in 1620. The mineral rights under the farm were spread amongst the Haslam family in the early 1800s but little detail is known of the mining operations.

The Levers held the east farm from 1660 until the freehold passed to the Jackson family by the marriage of Elizabeth Lever to Thomas Jackson of Liverpool in the late 1700s. Coal extraction from several pits was undertaken by the Levers in the first half of the 1700s but later workings were contracted to mining operators such as the Ormrods. The farm was eventually tenanted by James Haslam c1880.

In the Enclosures of 1797, Thomas Jackson was recorded as freeholder of Knotts East and Robert Haslam as holder of Knotts West.

(C) BROOKFOLD (North & South)

The first record we have of the Brooke (Brooks or Brookes) family of Harwood is William born c1560 and his wife Alis and it is their two eldest sons, Edmund and John, along with their descendants, who feature in the history of the farms over the next two centuries. (R20)

BROOKFOLD NORTH (Figures 19, 20 and 21) In 1607 the above Edmund held a lease from Sir Nicholas Mosley for 80 years at 6s.8d per annum. He had married Sarah Greenhalgh in 1601 and within the next decade the couple had produced four children, Margaret, Dorothy, George, and Edmund. When the Five Yeomen were selling the tenancies, Giles Ainsworth of Ainsworth bought the freehold of the farm for £38 as an appendage to his adjacent land holdings in Harwood. The Indenture dated 1615 was for *'messuages and lands in the hands of occupiers'*. The leasehold of occupant Edmund Brooke was retained and on his death in 1630 it descended to his eldest son George who, with his wife Ann, produced a family of four or more.

Figure 19 *Brookfold Farm (North).*
Occupied by Edmund Brooke in the 1500s but purchased by Giles Ainsworth in 1615. The Brookes 'recovered' the freehold from the Ainsworths in 1678.

Figure 20 *Brookfold Farm (North).*
Showing details of timber roof construction during refurbishment in 1986.

Figure 21 B*rookfold Farm (North).*
Showing details of internal wall framing during refurbishment in 1986.

Figure 22 *Brookfold Farm (South).*
John Brooke, Edmund's brother, purchased the farm in 1615. William Hulme
bought the freehold in 1664 but the Brookes remained in occupation.

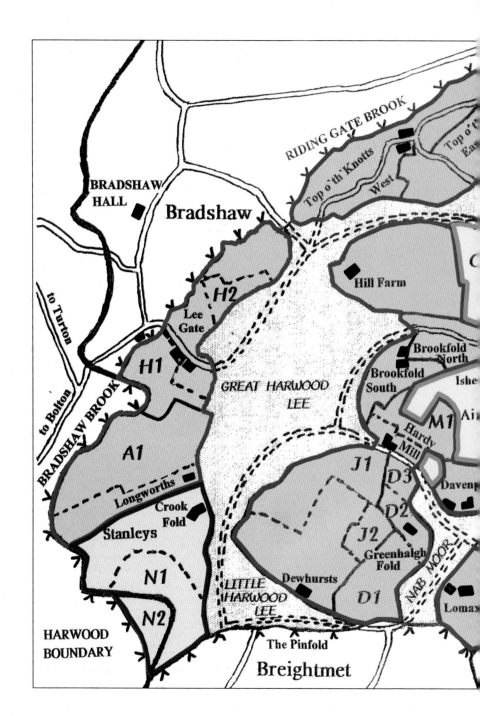

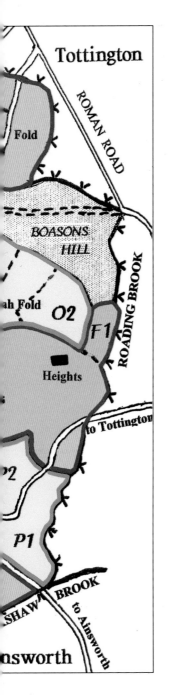

Early 'Splinter' Farms of the 1600/1700s.

A1 Longsight

D1 Goodwin Fold
D2 Pitfield
D3 Bryngs

F1 Hey Heads

H1 Lee Gate (East)
H2 Oxshutt Gate

J1 Hardy Mill Farm
J2 Harwood Meadows

M1 Heatons

N1 Shore
N2 Alders

O1 Hill End
O2 Higher Barn
O3 Castle

P1 Nab Fold
P2 Springfield

Figure 23 *Projected Map of Harwood c1600 showing the 'road' pattern and the boundaries of the farms and commons.*

41

The first son of George, Rev Edmund Brooke, was born in 1630 and he and his wife Fidelia had three children in the 1650s, Nathaniel, Edmund and Fidelia. The two sons had become chapmen before 1685 and established a business in Brownlow Fold, Little Bolton dealing mainly in textiles. Their sister Fidelia had married George Eskrick of Howden, Yorkshire in 1678 and they had five sons of which only two, Henry and Edmund survived.

Thirty years later about the time of George Eskrick's death, the two sons Henry and Edmund moved from Howden to Brownlow Fold to work in the thriving business with their uncles Nathaniel and Edmund. When the latter Edmund died in 1703 the business descended to his eldest son Cope who continued to run it in collaboration with his cousin Henry Eskrick.

Turning now to Benjamin Brooke, the second son of the above George, who was born in 1632 and succeeded to the farm about 1670. He and his wife Hannah had two sons, Samuel who took holy orders and became a vicar in Dorking, Surrey, and John who later tenanted and worked the adjacent Castle Farm. (more with Aspmah Fold)

In 1678 Benjamin procured the freehold of the farm from Jeremiah Ainsworth by a Common Recovery (R13) and rebuilt the house with the datestone 'B/BH/SB/1681' (Brooke/Benjamin-Hannah/Samuel Brooke/1681). Soon afterwards he bought Hawkeshutt House (eventually Oxshutt Gate Farm, Figure 36) located across the commons adjacent to Riding Gate Brook. To finance these transactions, Benjamin found it necessary to raise several mortgages and in his Will of 1692 he requested that *'my executors shall sell so many of my reall estates in Harwood ... to augment my personall estate ... to pay all my debts'*.

Rev Samuel inherited all his father's estate including Hawkeshutt House which on his death in 1698 descended to his cousin Edmund of Brownlow Fold and later to Edmund's son Cope. Samuel's Will of 1692 included a proviso that £400 should be settled with the church warden and overseer of the poor for Harwood. (see Goodwin and Brooke's Charity. Chapter V)

After Cope's death in 1732 the estate and business passed to Henry Eskrick by Letters of Administration and in 1738 he leased the two farms to Thomas Haslam for a period of 14 years at £32 pa. Over the years Henry Eskrick prospered and became a leading figure in the Halliwell area. (thus Eskrick Street) He was the Treasurer of Bolton School from 1740 until his death several years later.

By 1774 the two farms had been assigned to the Hulme Trust (but not Brasenose College) and were re-leased for a period of 21 years at an annual rent of £22 to the widow of John Bolton. In the Enclosures of 1797, Henry Eskrick's grandson, Henry, was recorded as the freeholder of both Brookfold North and Oxshutt Gate. The latter farm was rebuilt in 1800 alongside the old barn on the newly formed Boasons Hill Highway. (now Tottington Road)

BROOKFOLD SOUTH (Figure 22) John Brooke, the second son of William noted in the first paragraph of this account, occupied the south farm of about eight acres which he purchased from the five yeomen in 1616 for £32. He was recorded as a juryman at the *Inquisition post mortem* of Rowland Mosley and Richard Holland at the Manchester Court Leet in 1617 and 1619 respectively.

The farm descended to John's eldest son John who was the Constable for Harwood from 1654 to 1657. (see Chapter II) Later the estate passed to the latter John's eldest surviving son William who was born in 1636.

In 1664 William Hulme (Chapter VII) purchased the freehold of the farm from William Brooke, who at the time occupied it with his mother, and leased it back to him for a period of 99 years at an annual rent of 13s.8d. The lease included the unusual proviso: *'William Brooke ... shall yearly during the said term come unto the milne called Oakenbottom Milne with all his corn and graine ... to be ground .. as other tenants which grind their corn there'*. The Governors of Brasenose College were recorded as the freeholders of the farm in the Enclosures of 1797.

(D) GREENHALGH FOLD (Figure 24) (D1) Goodwin Fold (Figure 25
(D2) Pitfield (Figure 26) (D3) Bryngs (Figure 27)

The Greenhalgh family have been established in Harwood and Breightmet from as early as 1523 when Peter Greenhalgh is recorded as holding land from Edward Trafford. Two generations later his tenancy had descended to Edward Greenhalgh, one of the five yeomen, who purchased the freehold of the 20 acre farm for £74 from his four colleagues in 1617.

Edward had married Issabel Fogge in 1587 and they had eight children between 1588 and 1610: John, Elyn, Ester, Edward, Thomas, Issabel, Elizabeth and Katherine. Being *'a gentleman and freeholder of the manor'* (R2 & R8) he acted as juryman at the *Inquisition post mortem* of Richard Holland of Denton at the Mancheter Court Leet in 1619. Edward died in 1624 but his wife outlived him by some twenty-five years.

Their eldest son John, who like his father was a juryman in 1630, succeeded to the farm on his father's death and shortly afterwards proceeded to dispose of the

Figure 24 *Greenhalgh Fold.*
Held by the Greenhalgh family from as early as 1503. Purchased by
John Hough in the mid-1700s when the name changed to Hough Fold.

Figure 25 *Goodwin Fold. Originally part of Greenhalgh Fold.*
Acquired by Rev Richard Goodwin c1645 on his marriage to Sarah Crompton.

Figure 26 *Pitfield Farm 1981.*
Owned by John Hough from the mid-1700s.

Figure 27 *Bryngs Farm 1954.*
Built in 1721. Owned by the Governors of Queen Anne's Bounty for the
Curate of Walmsley Chapel who at the time was the colourful Parson Folds.

11 acres to the south of the estate. Seven fields were procured by James Crompton of Crompton Fold, Breightmet and five fields were purchased jointly by Joshua and John Lomax.

All these lands, along with a small field held by John Greenhalgh, subsequently came into the possession of the Rev Richard Goodwin by Indentures of 1645, 1673 and 1674 and later became known as Goodwin Fold. Richard had married Sarah, the daughter of James Crompton soon after his appointment as Vicar of Cockey Chapel (Ainsworth) in 1641. His nonconformist clerical activities were earlier reviewed in Chapter V. John Lomax of the adjacent Lomax Fold and Joshua Lomax of St Albans are noted later in the accounts of Lomax Fold and Hardy Cornmill.

After Richard Goodwin's death in 1685, the farm passed down through the Okeys, Cromptons and Jones', all noted nonconformist families of Bolton. It was purchased in 1790 by James Heywood of Bradley Fold who is recorded as the freeholder in the Enclosures of 1797. In 1849 the farm was acquired by Joseph Yates of Earls farm across Stitch mi Lane in Breightmet and later the Yates' built Goodwin House with a datestone of 1879 to accommodate the non-farming members of the family.

Turning now to the northern area retained by John Greenhalgh; this was later transferred to Thomas Thomasson of Edgworth by an Indenture of 1647. The farmstead at the time was occupied by John Greenhalgh and his mother, Arthur Bromiley and probably Thomas Thomasson who for many years was also the tenant farmer at Goodwin Fold.

In the mid 1700s John Hough purchased Greenhalgh Fold which had by that time gained two other small farms to the north of the estate, Pitfield and Bryngs. By an Indenture of 1782 Pitfield was leased by John Hough to Abraham Hardman of Westhoughton for a period of 999 years at an annual rent of £3.3s.

About the same period Bryngs on Hardy Mill Road was purchased by the Governors of Queen Anne's Bounty for the Curate of Walmsley Chapel who was noted as owner in the Enclosures of 1797. The curate at the time was the colourful Parson Folds, (Figure 55) a notable character in the Bolton area who concurrently held the Lectureship at Bolton Parish Church from 1755 to 1820. Bryngs farmhouse was at a later period a beerhouse named the Hen and Chickens.

In the Enclosures, John Hough was recorded as the freeholder of Greenhalgh Fold, or Hough Fold as it became known, and the farm was subsequently acquired by John Bolton, a corn and flour dealer of Bolton who on his death in 1879, left it to his son Robert.

(E) HOYLES FOLD (Figure 28)

The family of William and Margaret Saunderson, whilst originating in Breightmet, had close connections with Hoyles Fold and also Heights and Hill, the following two farms to be examined in this chapter. They had four children in the late 1500s: John who married Elizabeth Bromiley from Turton, Ellis who became the Vicar of Bolton, Margaret who married Raufe Higson (from Heights?) and Alice who married a man named Harrison. When father William died in 1601 he left one third of his estate to his wife Margaret, one third to be shared by son Ellis and daughter Margaret Higson and the remaining third to be divided between widowed daughter Alice Harrison, widowed daughter-in-law Elizabeth and others.

Son Ellis was instituted to the Vicariate of Bolton in 1598 and became an avid nonconformist as noted in Chapter I. When he died in 1625 all his children were under twenty-one and he left his smallholding of two acres (probably at Hoyles Fold) to his son Ellis to be *'kept in feoffees state unto his daye by two survivors - Laurence Horrockes and Mattheu Harison'*. Put simply, the land was to be held in trust, until Ellis became of age, by Lawrence Horrocks from Hill Farm, and Matthew Harrison.

Matthew Harrison who occupied Hoyles Fold was one of the five yeomen and he would have bought the 21 acre farm from the other four trustees c1615 for about £77. He was obviously a man of substance, being one of the four Harwood residents to pay the Lay Subsidy of 1625. When he died in 1633 his eldest son William succeeded to the farm which he sold three years later for £220 to John Higson (see Heights), the previous joint occupant. (Could there possibly have been a marriage link between Matthew Harrison and widow Alice Harrison-nee Saunderson?)

On John Higson's death in 1655 the farm descended to Thomas Bridge, the husband of his daughter Alice who sold 15 acres of the land to Thomas Lever of Chamber Hall for £100 by an Indenture of 1662. Thomas Bridge, Alice and son John continued to occupy the farm until 1674 but in 1669 the residual 6 acres were also sold to Thomas Lever for £40.

Thomas Lever then owned all Hoyles Fold along with Top o'th' Knotts Farm (East) which he had purchased in 1660. His descendants continued to hold the above estates until the 1880s and in the Enclosures of 1797 the freeholder of Hoyles Fold was recorded as Thomas Jackson, a Gentleman of Liverpool who had married into the Lever family.

Figure 28 *Hoyles Fold.*
The farm was occupied by Matthew Harrison in the early 1600s and later
held by the Lever Family of Bolton from 1674 until the 1880s.

Figure 29 *Heights Farm c1987.*
Matthew Fletcher, notable mining engineer and instigator of the Manchester,
Bolton & Bury Canal, acquired the farm in 1784 from the Flitcroft family.

(F) HEIGHTS (Figure 29) (F1) Hey Heads (Figure 30)

Whilst there is no documentary proof, it would seem likely that Raufe Higson, one of the five yeomen was the purchaser of Heights Farm from the other four trustees in the early 1600s. As noted in the previous account of Hoyles Fold, he had married Margaret Saunderson in 1597 and during the next decade the couple had four children, John, Priscilla, Margerie and Elizabeth, of whom the three daughters all died in infancy. Raufe is recorded as a juryman at the *Inquisition Post Mortem* of Rowland Mosley at Manchester Court Baron in 1617. He died c1625 and his wife Margaret died four years later. Shortly afterwards the surviving son, John, took up joint occupancy with William Harrison at Hoyles Fold which he eventually purchased.

By 1678 the freehold of Heights had been acquired by Michael Flitcroft, a merchant from Manchester who rebuilt the farmhouse (datestone MF 1678) and leased the farm to Richard Greenhalgh. The estate subsequently descended to his son Litchford who in his Will of 1760 left it to the six children of the late Peter Flitcroft of Farnworth. Various amounts were bequeathed to John, Peter, Alice and Catherine and *'the remainder of the estate ... was to be divided equally between Seth Flitcroft and Thomas Flitcroft their heirs and assigns forever'*.

A small farm, Hey Heads, of 3 acres with three cottages had been developed in the north-east corner of the estate which Seth Flitcroft later leased to John Warburton by an Indenture of 1782 for 999 years at £9.9s pa.

The husband of Catherine Flitcroft was the notable Matthew Fletcher who by an agreement of 1784 acquired the freehold of Heights from Seth Flitcroft and rebuilt some of the out-buildings, the farm at the time being tenanted by John Roscow. Matthew Fletcher was a mining engineer who had acquired the Wet Earth Colliery at Clifton in the 1750s. This was the first deep mine in the Irwell Valley and was subject to flooding from the Irwell Valley Fault. The mine was eventually drained with an ingenious pumping system devised by the up and coming hydro-engineer, James Brindley. Over the next century the Fletcher family became one of the largest coal mine operators in the Irwell Valley.

Matthew was also a leading figure in the promotion of the Manchester, Bolton & Bury Canal in 1790 preparing the initial survey and estimate of cost and supervising the construction with his nephew John Nightingale as Resident Engineer. He and his grand-nephew Ralph Fletcher of the Haulgh were appointed Commissioners for the Enclosure of Bolton Moor in 1792 and Ralph acted in a similar capacity for the Enclosure of Harwood Commons five years later. As a magistrate, Colonel Ralph Fletcher played a crucial role in the 'Peterloo Massacre' in St Peter's Field, Manchester in 1819.

In the Enclosures of Harwood, Matthew Fletcher was recorded as the freeholder of both Heights and Hey Heads Farms tenanted by John Roscow and Abram and James Warburton respectively.

(G) HILL (Figures 31,32 & 33)

In the late 1500s, Hill Farm was occupied by one of the five yeomen, namely Lawrence Horrocks from Ainsworth, and he would have purchased the freehold of the 25 acre estate for about £92 from his four colleagues during the conveyancing to the occupiers.

Lawrence and his wife had four children between 1591 and 1603, Allis, Robert, Elline and Thomas. On his death in 1641 the farm descended to his eldest son, Robert who was married twice and had a family of nine children between 1615 and 1639

We have little knowledge of the ownership of the farm over the next century but the Horrocks family apparently remained in occupancy until at least the end of the 1600s. John Horrocks is recorded in 1694 as encroaching on the commons with a close of 2 acres and Widow Hester Horrocks with a cottage. (A7)

In the mid 1700s the freehold of the farm was acquired, probably as an investment, by Sir Ashton Lever of Alkrington with Oliver Ormrod as tenant. The Ormrods were an ancient family from Cliviger near Burnley and the first member to arrive in Harwood was Oliver who married local girl Elizabeth Hill in 1703 and produced ten children.

When Oliver died in 1756 their eldest son Oliver re-leased the farm from Ashton Lever for the lives of his three sons John, Thomas and Oliver at a rent of four guineas per year. The tenancy then continued to pass down the male line of the Ormrod family with Thomas and later Oliver III.

Seven years after the death of Ashton Lever in 1787, Josiah Lancashire and Joseph Artingstal, both yeomen from Prestwich, acquired the farm from his devisees in trust and they are recorded as freeholders in the Enclosures of 1797 with Oliver Ormrod as tenant.

On the death of Oliver in 1831 the tenancy of the farm was inherited by his second cousin, Peter Ormrod. Peter was a very wealthy cotton manufacturer in the Bolton area who in the 1860s funded the rebuilding of the Parish Church *'entirely at his own cost'*. He purchased the freehold of the farm in 1835 and ten years later sold the mining rights to James Hardcastle of Firwood.

Figure 30 *Hey Heads Farm 1976.*
Developed by the Flitcroft family in the NW corner of the Heights Estate and
leased to John Warburton in 1782. Later held by Matthew Fletcher.

Figure 31 *Hill Farm 2002 (Now in ruins).*
Occupied by the Horrocks family during the 1600s. Eventually held by
Peter Ormrod who funded the re-building of Bolton Parish Church in 1866.

Figure 32 *Hill Farm 2000.*
Showing the timber framing to an internal wall.

Figure 33 *Hill Farm 1972.*
Showing the heck and bressumer beam framing to the chimney breast.
This form of first floor construction was peculiar to the area.

(H) LEEGATE (Figure 34) (H1) Leegate-Eastern (Figure 35)
(H2) Oxshutt Gate (Figure 36)

The original farm of about 27 acres situated at the gateway to Great Harwood Lee was in the possession of the Bromiley family for over three centuries and four of their menfolk, Thomas, William, Arthur and John are recorded as inhabitants of Harwood in the late 1500s.

Arthur Bromiley married Margery Bradshaw of the Birches, Bradshaw in 1605 and over the next fifteen years the couple reared a large family with John, Arthur, Thomas, Ellen, Margery and others. Arthur the father would have been the purchaser of the freehold of Leegate Farm from the five yeomen for about £100 and he was one of the four wealthier landholders of Harwood and Bradshaw liable to pay the Lay Subsidy (or tax) for the year 1622.

In the mid-1600s a small farm of about seven acres was established to the north of the estate named Hawkeshutt House (later Oxshutt Gate) which was acquired by Benjamin Brooke c1685. (see Brookfold North)

After passing down three further generations of Arthur, Leegate Farm descended to the fifth Arthur who was warden at Bolton Parish Church in 1729. On the barn built about that time is an unusual datestone (see Title Page) which reads: *'Arthur, Alis Bromelle 1729. And we know that if our earthly hous of this tabernacle be destroyed we have building given of God is an house not made with handes but eternall in heavens'*. (2 Corinthians. ch.5, v.1)

About 1750 another farmhouse was built to the east of the original farm and around the same time Leegate Farm Bleachworks was established by Samuel Hardman in the south-west corner of the estate adjacent to Riding Gate Brook. In the Enclosures of 1797 Daniel Wolstenholme of Manchester was recorded as the freeholder of the land with Jonathon Hardman as tenant. The bleachworks was dissolved towards the end of the century and put up for sale by Daniel Wolstenholme in 1810. On a site plan for the Public Health (Water) Act of 1878 the farm was titled Leegate (Eastern). (Now site of Library and Petrol Station).

In 1831 the original farmhouse and about fifteen acres of land south of Lee Gate were purchased by the Hardcastles of Bradshaw Bleachworks who in the 1850s developed the workers' community of King Street, Church Street etc in the north-west corner. All these holdings were transferred to the Bleachers' Association in 1900. (R21)

Thomas Bromiley remained in occupation as tenant farmer of the original farm and Thomas Hardcastle later added a barn with the datestone 'TH 1896'. The

Figure 34 *Leegate Farm c1910.*
Occupied by the Bromiley family for over three centuries and purchased by
the Hardcastles of Bradshaw Bleachworks in 1831.

Figure 35 *Leegate Farm (Eastern) c1935.*
Farm established in the mid-1700s and tenanted by the Hardman family.
The photograph shows the Howarth family who were recent tenants.

Figure 36 *Oxshutt Gate Farm June 1977.*
This farm was originally named Hawkeshutt House and located adjacent to
Riding Gate Brook. Rebuilt in 1800 alongside the old barn on Tottington Rd.

Figure 37 *Hardy Mill Farm c1910 (on the right).*
Developed by John Pilling about 1780. Sold in 1838 to Charles Hopwood
who subsequently owned Hardy Cornmill and Brookfold Lane Quarry.

farm was often referred to as Manor Farm for identification purposes and the farmhouse remains today as an unspoiled example of 17th century South Lancashire rural architecture.

(J) DEWHURSTS (J1) Hardy Mill Farm (Figure 37) (J2) Harwood Meadows

The Bromiley family featured in the previous account of Lee Gate Farm were widespread in Harwood during the 1600s and 1700s and it is considered from later documentary evidence that they held the large farm of about 42 acres to the south of the township later to be known as Dewhursts. John Bromiley, born c1580 would probably have been the purchaser of the farm for about £156 from the five yeoman.

By the mid-1600s a small farm of about 8 acres called Harwood Meadows had been developed on the eastern border of the estate and by a Final Concord (R13) of 1658 the freehold of this farm was passed by Thomas Bromiley (grandson of the above John) and others to James Isherwood of Isherwood Fold. It was later acquired by Meadowcroft Heaton who married into the Isherwood family in 1755 (see Isherwood Fold) and by a further Agreement of 1786 the farm passed to John Heaton, Meadowcroft's eldest son. The Bromiley family built the White Horse Inn (Figure 38) in the south-east corner of Little Harwood Lee in 1701, probably on land encroached from the commons. The hostelry had several other names (Axe and Steel; Kings Head; Shoulder of Mutton; Horse and Jockey) before acquiring its present title towards the end of the century. About 16 acres of the original farm were acquired c1780 by the Parker family from Breightmet but Joseph Bromiley remained in occupation for about ten years until the tenancy was taken by Thomas Dewhurst.

Also about 1780 John Pilling from Tottington established the 18 acre Hardy Mill Farm in the north of the estate across the way from the cornmill. (R22) John and his wife Agnes had a large family of eleven children of whom six emigrated to America in the 1830s. John died in 1820 and 18 years later his executors sold the farm to Charles Hopwood from Horwich who subsequently owned Hardy Cornmill and Brookfold Lane Quarry.

At a sale of 63 oak trees and 19 cyphers (trees of little value) at the original farm in 1791, Thomas Dewhurst, who combined farming with jobbing joinery around the district, was named as the tenant. In a leasing advertisement of 1829 the farm was described as an 'Excellent Grain & Milk Farm of 16 acres'.

In the Enclosures, Thomas Parker was holding the freehold of the farm now designated Dewhursts, John Pilling's Mortgagee held Hardy Mill Farm and John Heaton held Harwood Meadows.

Figure 38 *White Horse Inn early 1900s.*
Originally built by the Bromiley family in 1701 probably on land encroached
from the commons. It had several names before acquiring its present title.

Figure 39 *Davenport Fold c1950.*
Held by the Davenport family for over two centuries. The cottages to the left
were used as the Workhouse and Township Offices during the 1800s.

(K) DAVENPORT FOLD (Figure 39)

The marriage of John Damforte (modified to Davenport c1655) to Anne Gardiar was registered in 1592 and it would be John who purchased the freehold of what was later to become Davenport Farm from the five yeomen c1615 for about £30. The farm of about 8 acres was located along the northern boundary of Nab Moor and surrounded by the holdings of the Ainsworth family.

In the fourteen years after their marriage, John and Anne Davenport produced a small family of three children, Mary, John and Thomas, but it was Thomas who succeeded to the farm on his father's death in 1631. He and his wife Alice reared six children over the next decade, namely Mary, Elizabeth, Anne, John, Thomas, Ellin and Alice. The two sons, John and Thomas seem to have jointly worked the farm after their father's death in 1657 and they both later took up official duties in the district.

John Davenport, born 1637 was the Petty Constable for Harwood in 1657 but was recorded in 1694 as having encroached on the commons with one cottage. Thomas born 1638 was an Assessor for the Poll Tax of 1678 (A3) and is registered with *'wyfe and child'* in the tax returns. He and his wife Mirriam built a cottage on the end of the farmhouse bearing the datestone 'TMD 1681' (cemented over c1950.) and one of their sons, Thomas, was Overseer of the Poor for Harwood in 1729. In the Enclosures of 1797 the freehold of the estate was held by Mr Davenport's Devisees.

The fold had increased in size during the late 1700s with six cottages seemingly added to John Davenport's original cottage. Four of the cottages were inter-connected with doorways and used as the local workhouse until 1837 when the inmates were moved temporarily to Goose Cote Farm, Turton, and in 1861 to Fishpool, Bolton. In the 1841 Census five of the cottages were occupied by hand-loom weavers and the remaining two would probably be the Harwood Township Offices which were known to be located at Davenport Fold about that time.

The estate was up for sale in 1874 and purchased for nearly £2000 by John Bolton who had previously bought Hough Fold. (see Greenhalgh Fold) The sale included the farm with land yearly tenanted at a rent of £65 by Mrs Robinson and the row of seven cottages plus four others built later in the farmyard, all let at weekly rent. In 1903 a double fronted house in brickwork with a stone-faced frontage was built over two of the cottages which were subsequently dismantled.

(L) LOMAX FOLD (Figure 40) with Nab Gate (Figure 41)

John Lomax and his relative Joshua Lomax are recorded as jointly transferring land in Harwood in the early 1600s (see Greenhalgh Fold) and John would appear to have been the founder of the farm originally known as 'Owd Jacks'. He acquired Old Nans Farm just over the Harwood boundary in north Breightmet as a dowry on his marriage to the proprietor's daughter Elizabeth c1610.

Within the next few years John Lomax would be the purchaser of the freehold of Lomax Fold from the five yeomen for about £66 for 18 acres. After his death in 1664, the next in line to the estate was Richard who in 1653 was noted as being in attendance with his wife Esabell at the funeral of the illustrious Humphrey Chetham of Turton Tower.

For the next century the estate continued to descend down the male line of the Lomax's (mainly Richards) during which time the family prospered. Richard IV married Ellen Knowles of Eagley Bank in 1751 and he developed the farmhouse, then known as Lomax Fold, into a grand Georgian residence. A datestone on the new extension reads 'L-RE-1757'. (Lomax-Richard & Ellen).

In the 1797 Enclosures of Harwood, the next in line, Robert, a successful velveteen manufacturer, was allotted 1 acre of land on the south-east side of Stitch mi Lane and a plot of 4 acres located on the north side of Longsight, later the site of Springside Farm built c1820.

Robert II followed his father in cotton manufacturing and added the Stable Block in 1828; he also built the 'Retainers Cottages' across Stitch mi Lane c1830 to house the servants. Shortly after the Enclosures a new farmhouse (Home Farm - later Nab Gate Farm) was built in the north-western corner of the estate on the recently allotted land and adjoining the old barn and outbuildings. Robert II was a great benefactor to Christ's Church, donating the land on which it was built in 1840 and building the new school in 1848 on land from Earl's Farm given by the Earl of Derby.

The following properties were included in a sale by auction of the Lomax Estate in September 1872: Harwood Lodge, Nab Gate Farm & cottage, Church Meadow, Springside Farm, Old Nan's Farm, two houses on Stitch mi Lane, four houses on Tottington Road, two cottages & land at Ruins. James Lever, a wholesale grocer from Bolton, bought Lomax Fold in 1873 for about £5000 and lived there until 1893. He died at Thornton Hough on the Wirral in 1897 aged 87. He was the father of Lord Leverhulme (William Hesketh Lever) of Sunlight Soap fame.

Figure 40 *Lomax Fold Painting 1806 (later Harwood Lodge).*
Occupied by eight generations of the Lomax family. In 1873 the house was
sold to James Lever, the father of William Hesketh Lever. (Lord Leverhulme).

Figure 41 *Nab Gate Farm.*
Built in the early 1800s by Robert Lomax on allotted land adjoining the old
barn. Virtually rebuilt and converted into individual dwellings in 2004/5.

(M) HARDY CORNMILL (Figure 42) (M1) Heatons (Figure 43)

In the 1500s almost every township had a water-powered cornmill usually owned by the Manor and operated by an independent miller. Harwood was no exception and towards the end of the century Elys Hardier with his wife and three sons occupied the cornmill located in the centre of the township. (R22) The first registration at Bolton Parish Church of the Hardier (Hardyer, Hardi, Hardie, Hardy) family was the burial of Elys's wife in 1589.

The eldest of the three sons, Ellis, was church warden for Harwood in 1645 and he would have been the purchaser of the cornmill with 13 acres of land from the five yeomen for around £48. His youngest son William was an approved Bread-baker and Maltster for Harwood in 1653. (see Chapter II)

In 1676 James Heaton, a landed yeoman from Halliwell, purchased the mill and land and nine years later sold them to Joshua Lomax of St Albans (See Greenhalgh Fold) whose object was to settle an endowment on Bolton Parish Church. Shortly after his acquisition Joshua leased the estate back to James Heaton with an annual rent-charge of £7 for a term of 1000 years. (lease thus effectively freehold) The tenancy subsequently passed to son James Jnr who occupied Heatons Farm which had been developed on the eastern border of the estate c1685. He and his wife Margaret had eight children and in his Will of 1741 he left his eldest son Meadowcroft in trust to dispose of the mill and several estates and share the proceeds amongst the family.

It was 1745 before the farm and land were sold to John Kirkman from Ainsworth and at the same time David, James Heaton's third son, purchased the mill and three acres of land with the attendant rent charge of £7. David had already worked the cornmill for many years and he and his wife Margaret built Heatons cottage on Hardy Mill Road adjoining the kiln with the datestone H/D&M 1757. (existing)

When David Heaton died in 1784 he devised his estates to his three daughters: eldest daughter Elizabeth with husband John Walch inherited the mill and Heaton's Cottage: second daughter Alice with husband James Ormrod inherited the three acres of land (plus £7 rent charge) with the shippon and two cottages built c1780 to the west of the mill: youngest daughter Ann with husband Dennis Kirkman inherited Rose Cottage built c1780 to the east of the mill. In the Enclosures of 1797 the above three sons-in-law were recorded as freeholders of their various holdings.

When the eldest daughter's husband, John Walch, inherited the mill he was 47 years old and he, then his son David, continued to grind the corn by millstone

61

Figure 42 *Hardy Cornmill. c1600. (Artist's Impression)*
The water-mill was in operation for about three centuries. The Hardies were
millers from the 1500s, the Heatons from 1676 and the Walches from 1784.

Figure 43 *Heatons Farm c1960.*
Developed c1685 and occupied by James Heaton Jnr. In 1745 the Kirkmans
bought the farm which was later tenanted by the Entwistles c1780 to 1850.

and water power for the next 60 years. David remained a bachelor and when he died in 1847 at the age of 84, he left all his estate in trust to his *'esteemed friend Charles James Darbyshire'*. (the first Mayor of Bolton) The intention was to establish a Charity Trust to *'erect a Building for use as a School or Schools, Public Library and Reading Room for the general education and rational amusement of the inhabitants of the Township of Harwood and the neighbourhood thereof'*.

It was twenty years before the trust was formed and another five years before completion of 'Walsh's Educational Institute'. (Walch was changed to Walsh in the Trust Deed) The Institute provided accommodation for public meetings, ARP depot, library, art and craft classes, etc. and was a valuable and convenient amenity for the township for over 130 years until it sadly closed its doors in 2004. (Figure 44)

Charles Hopwood from Horwich acquired Hardy Mill Farm c1838 and also worked the quarry up Brookfold Lane. He later rented the redundant cornmill for use as a stone-yard and subsequently a wheelwright and blacksmith's shop. He was Guardian of the Poor for Harwood from 1844 until his death in 1874.

In 1908 James Brooke, an estate agent from Farnworth, purchased Heatons Farm along with the land and cottages to the east of the mill and the annual rent-charge of £7 initiated by Joshua Lomax in 1685 was finally extinguished with a freehold reversion by the transfer of consolidated stock valued £280 yielding $2^{1}/_{2}\%$.

(N) CROOK FOLD (Figure 45) (N1) Shore (N2) Alders

The deeds and documents to hand for this 48 acre holding of the Earl of Derby located in the south-west corner of the township record only the conveyances of the various cottages and gardens, and it has not been possible to relate the early transactions to any particular properties.

Francis Davenport, a chapman of Salford is recorded in 1682 as holding a leasehold tenancy from the Earl of Derby for the lives of his three sons, Richard, Thomas and Francis. On the death of the youngest son, Francis, the tenancy was acquired by the Crompton family and later inherited by spinster Margaret Loe.

During the 1700s the Crook family from Little Lever occupied the farm and by an Indenture of 1787 John Crook purchased the tenancy from Margaret Loe. On his death in 1821 he devised the lease to his sons James and John and in 1837, four years after the death of James, brother John sold it to the Markland family of Little Lever.

Figure 44 *Walsh's Educational Institute.*
Bequeathed in 1845 by David Walch, the last miller. Built by the Trustees of
his Charity in 1872 (Walch was changed to Walsh in the Trust Deed).

Figure 45 *Crook Fold c1950.*
The lease of the farm was bought by John Crook in 1787.
The shippon/barn to the right remains as Bolton Open Golf Club.

Hey Knott Shore (Eye Not, Heynot, Hynot, High Knoll, etc.) was normally referred to as simply Shore Farm. It had been established in the mid 1700s with Ralph Greenhalgh and Robert Thomason as early tenants. In 1845 it was recorded as a licensed house and occupied by Samuel Heys.

The farmland of the estate would appear to have been leased separately from the properties on some periodic rental basis and in the Enclosures of 1797 the freeholds of both Crook Fold and Shore Farm were held by the Earl of Derby. During the 1800s Crook Fold was farmed by Samuel Bridge and later James Markland who incorporated the farmland of Shore Farm.

Little is known about Alders, a small farm of about 6 acres positioned on the south-west side of Bradshaw Brook, except that it was acquired in the early 1800s by James Hardcastle of the adjacent Firwood Bleach Works, for use as a beetling room powered by water wheel.

Both Crook Fold and Shore Farm were acquired c1885 by Harwood Vale Bleach Works who used the farm buildings to stable their cart-horses. After their amalgamation into the Bleachers' Association in 1900 [later Whitecroft Holdings Ltd. (R21)] the company maintained the tenancies of the farmers on a yearly lease and rental basis. The converted shippon/barn of Crook Fold remains as the clubhouse for the recently established Bolton Open Golf Complex.

(O) ASPMAH FOLD (Figure 46) (O1) Hill End (Figure 47)
(02) Higher Barn (Figure 48) (03) Castle (Figure 49)

The original Aspmah Fold of around 35 acres was located in the north of the Harwood holdings of the Ainsworths which later passed to the Hulme Trust. (R18).

Richard Aspinall, who occupied the farm in the early 1600s, married Alis Knowles in 1602 and they produced eight children over the next 22 years. He was a juryman in 1630 at the *Inquisition post mortem* of Stephen Pooley, a former Borough-Reeve of the Manor of Manchester. When Richard died in 1637 the farm descended to his youngest and only surviving son Richard, born 1612, who with his wife Margaret had a family of five children. A later Richard Aspinall was the Overseer of the Poor for Harwood in 1700 and died four years later.

The Aspinall family held their tenancy from the Hulme Trust *'at will without privity'* which meant their holding was implied, mutually terminable and non-assignable. In 1709 Thomas Aspinall held a lease for 20 years at a annual rent of £6 but in a Valuation Report of the Hulme Trust in 1776 the Aspinalls were accused of profiteering by having sold off the whole of their tenancy in four parcels without authorisation.

Figure 46 *Aspmah Fold 1983.*
The Aspinall family held the tenancy during the 1600s and Richard Aspinall was the Overseer of the Poor for Harwood in 1700.

Figure 47 Hill End Farm 1982.
Built in 1727 on part of the Aspmah estate. Tenanted by
William Horrocks and his son James who had a combined life span of 187 years.

Figure 48 *Higher Barn Farm 1976.*
Developed from an out-station barn of Aspmah Fold and tenanted by the
Roscow family from around 1780 to 1850.

Figure 49 *Castle Farm 2003.*
Originally part of the Aspmah estate. The farm was tenanted by the Brookes
from the Brookfold Farms from the early 1600s to the mid-1700s.

The first of these subtenancies was Castle Farm of about 11 acres occupied by John Brooke from Brookfold South. After John's death in 1645 the farm passed down the family to John, the son of Benjamin Brooke from the adjoining Brookfold North. John was Overseer of the Poor for Harwood in 1684 and on his death in 1703 he left various amounts to his children and named son Robert as holding Castle. In the mid-1700s the farm was occupied by the Haslam family until purchased by Rev Hampson about 1790. A much later Sale Notice of 1878 noted that it had been previously bought by James Ormrod, brother of Peter Ormrod from Hill Farm.

The second subtenancy was Hill End, a small farm of about 6 acres, built and occupied in 1727 by William Horrocks from Bradshaw. He was born in 1657 and when a widower at the age of 86 he married his housekeeper Elizabeth aged 28. A year later they produced a son James who subsequently occupied Hill End until shortly before his death in 1844. It is well chronicled elsewhere that the 187 year combined life span of William and son James stretched from the time of Oliver Cromwell to the reign of Queen Victoria.

Little is known about Higher Barn, the third farm of about 10 acres which was developed from an out-station barn on the north-west boundary of the Aspmah estate. It was tenanted by the Roscow family from around 1780 to 1850. In the Enclosures of 1797, Brasenose College held the freeholds of Aspmah and Higher Barn, James Horrocks held Hill End and Rev James Hampson held Castle.

(P) ISHERWOOD FOLD (Figure 50) (P1) Nab Fold (Figure 51)
(P2) Springfield (Figure 52)

Originally, Isherwood Fold was a farm of some 47 acres located in the south of the Harwood holdings of the Ainsworth family and eventually the Hulme Trust (R18). An early tenant, William Isherwood, was buried within Bolton Parish Church in 1593 and the family were well noted in records of Harwood inhabitants in the 1600s. James Isherwood born c1570 was a juryman at the *Inquisition post mortem* of Richard Holland at Manchester Court Leet in 1619. As related in the account of Dewhursts Farm, James Isherwood, a nephew of the above James, had acquired the freehold of Harwood Meadows in 1678 from Thomas Bromiley.

The tenancy of Isherwood Fold seems to have remained with the Isherwood family for about two centuries until 1755 when Ann Isherwood married Meadowcroft Heaton who was the eldest of the eight children of James and Margaret Heaton of Hardy Cornmill. He was born in 1695 and first married in 1722 to Elizabeth Fletcher of Ringley. In 1745 he was described as a schoolmaster of Pilkington. (R21)

Figure 50 *Isherwood Fold 1976.*
The farm seems to have been tenanted by the Isherwood family from the
mid-1500s to 1752 when it passed to Meadowcroft Heaton by marriage.

Figure 51 *Nab Fold Farm 1989.*
Rebuilt in 1737, the farm was earlier part of Isherwood Fold estate. A later
tenant, Lincoln Tootill was the 'most famous Water Diviner in NW England'.

There were four children from his two marriages, John, Charles, Thomas and Margaret. With his marriage to Ann he acquired all the Isherwoods' holdings and when he died in 1760 he left to his children the estates of Isherwood Fold, Nab Fold and Harwood Meadows, plus Old Pit and three houses in Bolton.

Nab Fold, a farm of about 12 acres established in the south-west corner of the estate was leased to John Mangnall in 1774 for 21 years at a rent of £12.12s pa. The Mangnalls had been recorded in Harwood in the late 1600s and it was most likely a descendant who rebuilt the farmhouse in 1837 with the datestone 'TM Esquire'. A much more recent tenant of Nab Fold was the notable Lincoln Tootill who in 1908 was described in Thomson's Weekly News as *'The most famous Water Diviner in the North of England'*: his wife Bertha ran a tea-room at the farm.

Springfield, a farm of about 15 acres, was developed by the Seddon family about the same time in the south-east of the estate with a farmhouse bearing the datestone 'MS 1763'. The detached 2 acre plot of land between Hardy Mill and Davenport Fold (Figure 23) was let out over the years to local farmers such as James Heaton and Arthur Bromiley, but in 1774 the Hulme Trust complained that sublettings were providing Rights of Common to farmers from other townships. In the Enclosures of 1797 the freeholds of Isherwood Fold and Nab Fold were held by the Governors of Brasenose College and Springfield Farm was held by Thomas Seddon's Assignees.

Figure 52 *Springfield Farm 1939.*
The farm was developed on the Isherwood Fold estate by the Seddon family and bears the datestone MS 1763. The barn is now part of Harwood Golf Club.

Chapter IX   INTO THE NINETEENTH CENTURY

The First National Census of 1801 returned a population of 1281 for Harwood, an increase of over a thousand in two centuries. To house this growth, extra dwellings had been built at several of the farms and folds examined in the previous pages and small communities had evolved at Riding Gate, (Figure 56) the Ruins, (Figure 57) and Bottom o'th' Moor. (Figure 58)

With the Enclosures of 1797 a third more land became available to the freeholders and the first 6″ Ordnance Survey of the district in 1845 showed that development had already commenced on some of the allotted land in the areas of Seven Stars, Longsight, Kay Fields and Stitch mi Lane. Four new farms had also been established with Pawsey Bank, Raikes, Springside and Down Green.

Five new roads were created within the bounds of the commons, three of which were main thoroughfares named Little Lee, Boasons Hill and Hardy Mill Highway. These roads, now renamed Stitch mi Lane, Tottington Road and Longsight/Hardy Mill Road respectively form the main routes through the township. The other two roads, Stone Pit Lane and Occupation Road, (now Brookfold Lane and Longsight Lane) connected the farms to the new Hardy Mill Highway. (Figure 53)

Major improvements for travelling further afield were inaugurated around the turn of the century. The Little Bolton to Edenfield Turnpike Road passing through Bradshaw opened c1800 and continued as a toll road until 1876. The Manchester, Bolton & Bury Canal was completed in 1790 establishing links with Bury Bridge and the Mersey & Irwell Navigation (later Manchester Ship Canal) and thus the Port of Liverpool.

In 1828 the Bolton to Leigh Railway opened connecting Bolton with the Leeds/Liverpool and Bridgewater Canals at Leigh and two years later with George Stephenson's newly constructed Manchester to Liverpool Railway at Kenyon Junction. The Bolton to Blackburn Railway was completed in 1847 providing local stations at the Oaks and Bromley Cross.

Surprisingly, during the industrial upsurge of the 1800s, the population of Harwood only increased by about 300 inhabitants. At the beginning of the century three quarters of the populace were engaged in the cottage industry of spinning and hand-loom weaving and the partnership of Lee & Hammery were producing hand-made shawls in a little brick built factory at the Ruins. Hand weaving gradually declined over the century and the first water powered looms in the district were operated in 1848 by Zachariah Nuttall in a small weaving shed on Folly Brook south of Hardy Mill Road.

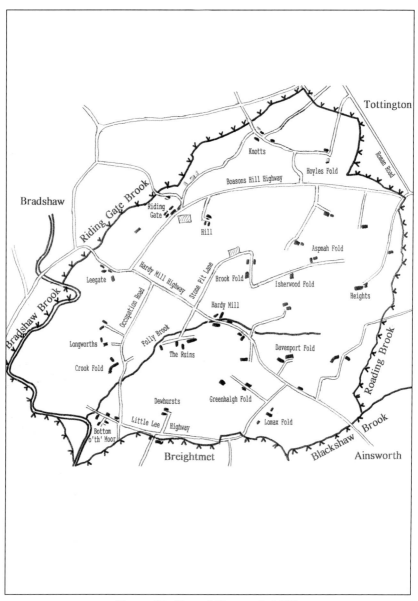

Figure 53 *Plan of Harwood c1800.*
The township after the Enclosures of 1797.
Note the new highways and occupation roads. Also the communities of
Riding Gate, the Ruins and Bottom o'th' Moor.

72

Later industrial ventures in the township included the Harwood Spinning Company who operated their four storey Prospect Mill on Hardy Mill Road from 1852 to 1886 and the Harwood Vale Bleachworks started in 1870 by Nathan Ramsden from Breightmet. In the mid-1800s Brookfold Quarry was being operated by Charles Hopwood from Hardy Mill Farm and several coal pits in the vicinity of Tottington Road were being worked by the Haslam, Scowcroft and Hardcastle families.

Ecclesiastical administration of the area was transferred from Chester to the newly created Diocese of Manchester in 1847 and soon afterwards the local parishes were separated but not as advocated in 1650. (R16) A three-fold growth in population over the two centuries had made it necessary to create three new parishes of which the Parish of Bradshaw was established in 1853 and the Parishes of Harwood and Tonge-cum-Breightmet followed in 1857.

The first 'church' in Harwood was the Wesleyan Chapel/School built in 1822 on Longsight. Christ's Church was the next to be established in 1840, being licensed initially for baptisms and burials only but with a license for marriages following six years later; their school for 150 pupils was built in 1848 on the opposite side of Stitch mi Lane. Tottington Road Primitive Methodist (Hephsibah Chapel) was opened in 1841.

No records or minutes have been traced of the Harwood Township Meetings which are known to have taken place from at least the second half of the 1600s. The meetings were held in the Township Office at Davenport Fold in the early 1800s and later in taverns such as the 'Britannia' on Tottington Road. In an attempt to move the meetings away from the beer houses, one was held at Walsh's Institute in 1874 but this was the only instance recorded.

The development of today's Harwood really took off after World War II. The lands (including enclosure allotments) of four of the original farms, namely Leegate, Dewhursts, Greenhalgh Fold and Davenport Fold, were completely covered with housing, shops and schools, Isherwood Fold and part of Heights Farm were converted into Harwood Golf Course and Crooks and Longworths were developed into Longsight Park, with Bolton Open Golf Course following in 1995. Fortunately, the remaining farms experienced hardly any development at all.

Since 1951 the population of Harwood has almost trebled to a figure of 4500, all the industry (except quarrying) has disappeared and the township remains as a residential suburb of Bolton maintaining a small amount of agriculture.

Figure 54
*Parish Church
of Bolton.
Demolished
1866.*

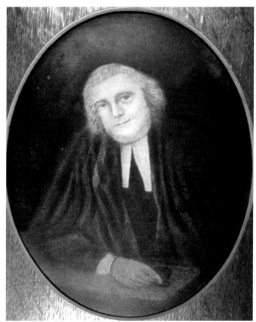

Figure 55
*Parson Folds 1728-1820
Lecturer of Bolton, Curate
of Walmsley Chapel &
Vicar of West Hythe, Kent.*

APPENDICES

A1 PROTESTATION RETURNS FOR HARWOOD 1641

Richard Barler
Robert Barler
Richard Battersby
Henery Birtwisle
Richard Booth
James Bradley
Raph Bridge
Thomas Bridge
Arthur Bromiley
Arthur Bromiley
Ellis Bromiley
William Bromiley
William Bromiley
Alexander Brooke
Ellis Brooke
George Brooke
John Brooke
John Brooke
John Brooke
Richard Brooke
James Crompton
James Crompton
John Crompton
Roger Crompton
Roger Crompton
Roger Crompton
Roger Crompton
Thomas Crompton
William Crompton
Thomas Davenport
Raph Entwisley
Adam Greenhalgh
John Greenhalgh
Richard Greenhalgh
William Greenhalgh
George Halliday
Thomas Halliday
Ehud Hardie
Ellis Hardie
William Hardie
Willyam Hardie
Richard Hardie

Adam Haslome
Ellis Haslome
Richard Haslome
Robert Haslome
John Higson
Anthony Holme
James Holme
James Holme
John Holme
Raph Holme
Richard Holme
Thomas Holme
James Holt
James Holt
James Horrocks
Robert Horrocks
James Isherwood
James Isherwood
John Isherwood
William Isherwood
John Kershaw
Richard Lomax
John Lowe
John Medowcroft
James Muchell
James Muchell
John Mutchell
Michael Mutchell
William Nabb
Richard Readman
Richard Roskoe
James Sanderson
John Sanderson
Edward Sidale
Roger Sidale
Richard Slater
Thomas Tonge
James Torner
William Vickers
Thomas Welch
Adam Woofenden
John Woofenden

Lancashire Record Office, Preston

A2 HEARTH TAX RETURNS HARWOOD 1664

CHARGEABLE

Widow Ashworth	1
Richard Aspinall	2
John Bridge	1
Thomas Bridge	1
Arthur Bromiley	1
Widow Bromiley	1
George Brooke	2
John Brooke	2
Widow Brooke	1
William Brooke	1
Widow Dampford	1
Thomas Fell	1
Mr Goodwin	2
John Greenhalgh	1
William Hardey	2
Widow Higson	1
Thomas Holmes	2
John Hough	1
John Hulton	1
James Isherwood	1
James Isherwood	1
John Isherwood	1
James Longworth	1
John Lomax	2
Thomas Lomax	1
William Taylor	1
Thomas Tonge	1
William Vickers	1

NOT CHARGEABLE

Edmund Barlow	1
Arthur Bromiley	1
Ellis Bromiley	1
George Bromiley	1
John Bromiley	2
Thomas Bromiley	1
William Bromiley	1
John Brooke	1
Richard Brooke	1
Widow Brooke	1
Roger Crompton	1
Roger Crompton	1
Widow Entisely	1
Widow Fogg	1
Thomas Hardey	1
William Hardey	1
Adam Haslom	1
Alice Haslom	1
Edmund Haslom	1
George Haslom	1
James Haslom	1
Thomas Horridge	1
Christopher Horrocks	1
Mary Hulton	1
Thomas Hurst	1
John Isherwood	1
Lawrence Manley	1
Thomas Meadowcroft	1
James Nuttall	1
John Orrill	1
Richard Roscow	1
Thomas Roscow	1
Widow Seedall	1
George Slater	1
Richard Slater	1
Widow Tonge	1
Arthur Turner	1
Widow Warburton	1
Thomas Wolsenham	1

Total No Hearths	**35**	Total No Hearths	**40**

Lancashire Record Office, Preston

A3 POLL TAX RETURNS FOR HARWOOD 1678

Imprimis the Hamlett of Harwood

Richard Aspinall & two Children
Isabell Meyo Maydservant
Richard Bradshaw
Arthur Bromiley his Wyfe & one Child
Jane Bromiley Widow
William Bromiley, his Wyfe & Child
Benjamin Brookes, his Wyfe & Child
John Brookes, his Wyfe & three Children
John Brookes Jnr & his Wyfe
Richard Brookes & his Wyfe
William Brookes & his Wyfe
William Brookes & his Wyfe
Ralph Crompton & Sister Alice Crompton
Alice Davenport Widdow
Richard Entwisle
William Entwisle
Richard Goodwin for a £100
Mary Massey his Maydservant
Lydia Haslom & Sister Elizabeth Haslom
Edmund Haslom & John Haslom
Robert Haslam, his Wyfe & Child
Ellis Haworth
James Heaton, his Wyfe & two Children
His Maydservant
William Holland & his Wyfe
Thomas Holme & his Wyfe

Thomas Hardman his Manservant
Peter Horridge
John Hough, his Wyfe & Child
John Hulton, his Wyfe & two Children
James Isherwood, his Wyfe & Child
William Isherwood & his Wyfe
John Leystar & his Wyfe
Elizabeth Lomax
Thomas Lomax
Widow Longworth & two Children
Katherine Roscow Maydservant
Thomas Mangnell & Bro Reneld Mangnell
Thomas Meadowcroft
Thomas Meadowcroft, his Wyfe & Child
Mary Norberry
Samuell Openshaw
John Roscow
William Roscow
Thomas Sharrocke & his Wyfe
George Slater & his Wyfe
Adam Stanton & one child
Anne Sudall
Mary Sweetlove & three Children
John Welch & his Wyfe
Edward Wood, his Wyfe & Child
Thos Davenport, Wyfe & Child. Assessor
Richard Masson & his Wyfe. Assessor

The above list includes five people who were originally assessed but chose to appeal against it and their appeal was granted. They were Richard Brookes & his wyfe, Jane Bromiley a poor widow, Thomas Mangnell & Bro Reneld Mangnell.

Lancashire Record Office, Preston

A4 HARWOOD WILLS AT CHESTER

1592	Roger Crompton	1725	Arthur Bromiley chapman	1821	Peter Crook farmer
1592	John Greenhalgh	1725	Thomas Gibbons	1822	Alice Ormrod widow
1592	Robert Haslam	1725	Thomas Heton weaver	1824	John Walch
1592	William Haslam	1726	Makepeace Mason yeoman	1824	Richard Scowcroft
1603	William Haslam	1727	John Sharples yeoman	1824	James Coop millwright
1609	Geoffrey Rishton	1728	William Alston yeoman	1824	Joseph Hamer tanner
1612	John Knowles	1728	Alice Mason widow	1826	Samuel Bromiley yeoman
1616	Edward Wilkinson	1728	John Robertshaw	1829	William Bridson bookkeeper
1617	Lawrence Crompton	1728	James Longworth yeoman	1830	William Nuttall farmer
1617	John Hindle	1728	George Tonge weaver	1830	Robert Greenhalgh innkeeper
1623	Henry Haworth	1732	James Seddon	1831	Ann Ramwell widow
1630	Edmund Brooke (missing)	1733	John Bolton yeoman	1832	Margaret Thweat
1637	Richard Aspinall	1740	Thomas Aspinall yeoman	1834	Thomas Heywood weaver
1637	Wm Greenhalgh yeoman	1741	James Heaton yeoman	1835	James Bromiley weaver
1641	John Mason	1742	Thomas Holmes yeoman	1835	George Heaton yeoman
1641	Ralph Bridge gentleman	1745	Thomas Holme whitster	1835	Samuel Horrocks farmer
1663	John Davenport	1749	Thomas Haslam sawyer	1837	John Howarth yeoman
1664	John Lomax Elton	1749	Arthur Bromiley chapman	1838	John Pilling yeoman
1669	Susan Clayton widow	1753	Richard Barlow weaver	1840	Robert Haslam weaver
1670	Willam Clayton	1756	John Lomax yeoman	1840	John Howarth farmer
1670	Thomas Fell	1757	Oliver Ormrod yeoman	1842	James Horrocks farmer
1672	William Mason	1760	Meadowcroft Heaton	1843	Ellen Hopwood
1672	Susanna Mason	1777	John Roscoe yeoman	1844	Peter Ackerley weaver
1675	John Clayton	1778	John Entwistle mason	1844	Thomas Bromiley weaver
1677	Jane Clayton/Whatley	1779	Richard Lomax	1845	Robert Walsh farmer
1680	George Harper yeoman	1780	Richard Haslam plasterer	1847	David Walch miller
1685	Jane Ratcliffe	1786	William Lomax miner	1848	Edward Whittle farmer
1686	Richard Goodwin	1790	Abraham Hardman	1851	Rachael Heaton widow
1686	Margery Longworth	1797	John Greenhalgh	1851	James Kay dealer
1687	Thomas Davenport	1798	Mary Hardman widow	1851	Margaret Lomax spinster
1691	John Cunliffe	1800	Thomas Roberts clothier	1852	Ann Haslam spinster
1692	Benjamin Brookes yeoman	1803	Oliver Ormrod yeoman	1853	John Haslam yeoman
1693	Holcroft Peele widow	1806	Ellis Walsh farmer	1853	Samuel Bridge
1699	Ralph Crompton weaver	1809	Robert Haslam yeoman	1853	John Nuttall farmer
1699	Richard Aspinall yeoman	1810	Dolly Walsh widow	1856	John Nightingale gent
1700	Mary Holmes widow	1811	Abraham Haslam yeoman	1856	Joseph Parker farmer
1700	Ann Clayton	1812	John Thweat yeoman	1856	George Warburton labourer
1702	John Cowper	1812	Thomas Smith yeoman	1857	Thomas Leach labourer
1703	Robert Bolton	1814	Reginald Ramsbottom		
1703	John Brookes of Castle	1814	John Coop carpenter		
1704	Richard Aspinall yeoman	1814	Mary Hamer widow		
1704	Thomas Clayton	1815	John Thweat bleacher		
1717	Robert Cunliffe	1815	Michael Haworth yeoman		
1719	Richard Sudell yeoman	1815	Robert Lomax cotton mnfr		
1720	John Morley yeoman	1816	James Morton cotton mnfr		
1720	Thomas Meadowcroft	1818	John Haslam weaver		
1724	Richard Mason yeoman	1819	Ellis Greenhalgh bleacher		

*This list is extracted from
'Bolton Wills at Chester 1545-1858'
by J C Scholes and covers the period
from the foundation of the Ecclesiastical
Court of Chester to the institution of the
Probate Registry. It is not presented as
a complete record.*

A5 TITHE COMMISSIONER'S REPORT   30th November 1854

WHEREAS an Award or Rent Charge in lieu of Tithes in the Townshp of Harwood in the Parish of Bolton Le Moor in the County of Lancaster was duly confirmed by the Tithe Commissioners for England and Wales on the Twenty Eighth Day of November, One Thousand Eight Hundred & Forty Four.

AND WHEREAS by the said Award the annual sum of Three Pounds, Six shillings & Eight pence was Awarded to be paid by Rent Charge to the Lord Bishop of Chester and the Right Honourable George Augustus Frederick Henry Earl of Bradford and his lessee in lieu of the Tithes or Payments instead of Tithes to which the said Bishop and his said lessee were entitled in the said Township.

AND WHEREAS the said paid Rent Charge has not been apportioned.

AND WHEREAS application was made to the said Tithe Commissioners in persuance of the Statute of 9 and 10 Victoria cl.73 that the said Rent Charge might be redeemed and the said Commissioners fixed the sum of Eighty Pounds as the proper amount to be paid for the redemption of such Rent Charge being not less than Twenty Four times the amount thereof.

AND WHEREAS the said Bishop of Chester and the said Earl of Bradford the persons entitled to the rump of the paid Rent Charge have signified their consent to such redemption upon the terms aforesaid.

AND WHEREAS under and by virtue of the provision of the said Statute of the said Tithe Commissioners have duly nominated Charles Thomas Wakefield Bishop of Chester, gent, John Simpson of London and John Shaw of London, gents, to be Trustees into whose hands the said sum of Eighty Pounds shall be paid and the said Charles Thomas Wakefield, John Simpson and John Shaw as such Trustees have given an acknowledgment under their hands that the said sum of Eighty Pounds has been received by them to be applied as directed by the said Statute.

NOW WE the undersigned Tithe Commissioners for England and Wales in consideration of payment of the sum of Eighty Pounds in manner aforesaid and by virtue of the powers vested in us by the said Statute do hereby certify that the said Rent Charge of Three pounds, Six shillings & Eight pence has been redeemed and that the said Township of Harwood is discharged of the said Rent Charge and of the said Tithes and Payments in lieu of tithes instead of which such Rent Charge was Awarded to be paid from the Twentieth Day of October, One Thousand Eight Hundred & Fifty Four.

IN TESTIMONY WHEREOF we have hereby inscribed our respective names and caused our official seal to be affixed this Thirtieth Day of November, One Thousand Eight Hundred & Fifty Four.

Manchester Local Studies L95/1

A6 SURVEY OF THE COMMONING OF HARWOOD 1694

A True Survey taken of ye Commoning of Harwood & Bradinge & Boundaries thereof, upon view & inquiry of ye Incroachm[en]ts & inclosures made by ye severall Persons & in ye Descriptions & Occupations of ye Persons hereafter named.

John Grosnell from Bitter Sweet Wood in meadow Hedge to Harwood Stud. Ralph Crompton of Harwood, & incroachm[en]t of ground & one House, a Garden, Shippon & Stable.

George Haslem & Ann Crompton & Cottages & a Garden. Edmund Haslem one Messuage & ... James Mutchill one House. Allice Howorth one House & fields one Acre. James Longworth & little Buildings. Abraham Rescot one field & Acre. Thomas Hanson one Inclosure for Lee Pitts one field one Barn one garding, one Messuage, one Barn & all one Acre. Thomas Ett one Messuage & Garden. Ralph Entwisle one House Garden & Shippon. James Healon one Day & ... John Howroe one Messuage, one ... & Acres. Ellis Howroe Widow one Cottage. Richard Entwisle one Messuage, one Garden. John Bradshaw one Messuage, one Cottage, one garden, one Acre of Land. Thomas Ett one Messuage & ... Thomas Horridge one Messuage one Garden. John Bridge one Cottage. John Davenport one Messuage, or one Cottage. ... Holmes one Cottage & one Garden. John Hague one Close & Acres. ... one Messuage & a Garden.

Freeholders & Charterers & ye Owners & Commoning in Harwood in ye Parish of Bolton in ye County of Lancast[er]. This 1[s]t of April 1694. James Jordan. Michael Ridiont. Robert Lees. Thomas Lees. Samuel Brookes. John Jones. John Banks. Richard Comax. Thomas Hulme. Thomas ....

The Names of ye Trustees of Bolton School

The Names of ye Trustees of ... Chappell.

The said Trustees: James ...worth. James Healon. John Hague. Arthur Bromley & John Davenport.

Whether these ... be laid upon or in a warrant for ejectm[en]t, because they have also considerable Lands in ye Township having inclosed part of ye Common.

For Pinners for ye Common   Richard Comax. George Haslem. Michael Mutchill.

Widow Brooks.	William Usherwood.
Widow Ratt.	Robert Blundive.
William Davenport.	Widow Rescot.
John Hague.	William Rescot.
James Hockman.	George Taylor.
Thomas Croft.	Walk Mill.
Richard Aspinall.	
Ellis Walch.	These are itt [th]ey whether
John Allen.	[th]ey have any Land's in Harwood

A7 *A true survey taken of the commoning of Harwood and leading the Boundaries thereof upon view and inquiry of the incroachments and inclosures made by the several persons and in the possessions & occupations of the persons hereafter named.*

John Greenall From Bitter Sweet Tree in Meadow Hedge to Harwood Stud.
Ralph Crompton of Harwood, two incroachments of ground, and one house, a
garden, shippon & stable.
George Haslam & Ann Crompton Two cottages & a garden.
Edmund Haslam One messuage, two closes, one acre.
James Mutchill One house.
Alice Howorth One house, two fields, one acre.
James Longworth Two little buildings.
Abraham Roscoe One field, half acre.
Thomas Hamer One inclosure for Tan pitts, one field, barn, garden, messuage -
all one acre.
Thomas Lee One messuage & garden.
Ralph Entwistle One house, garden & shippon.
James Heaton One bay & toft.
John Horrox One messuage, one close, two acres.
Ester Horrox widow One cottage.
Richard Entwistle One messuage & garden.
John Bradshaw One messuage, one cottage & garden, one acre of land.
Thomas Settle One messuage, half acre of land.
Thomas Horridge One messuage & garden.
John Bridge One cottage.
John Davenport One messuage or one cottage.
Eliz Hulme One cottage & one garden.
John Hague One close, two acres.
Arthur Bromeley One messuage or a garden.

Trustholders & Charterers of the Commons in Harwood in the Parish of Bolton in the County of Lancaster. 10th April, 1694.

James Cheetham, Michael Flitcroft, Robert Lever, Thomas Lever, Samuel Brookes, John Grundy, John Brookes, Richard Lomax, Thomas Hulme, Thomas Meadowcroft.

The names of the Feoffes of Bolton School
The names of the Feoffes of Cockie Chappell

These have inclosed: James Longworth, James Heaton, John Hague, Arthur Bromeley, John Davenport. Whether these five may be distrained upon or in a warrant for ejectment because they have other considerable lands in the Township having inclosed part of the Common.

For Pinners for the Common: Richard Lomax, George Haslam, Michael Mutchill.

Widdow Brookes, Widdow Nabs, William Davenport, John Hague, James Kirkman, Thomas Croft, Richard Aspinall, Ellis Walch, John Allen, William Usherwood, Robert Blundies, Widdow Roscoe, William Roscoe, George Taylor, Walk Mill. These are ith'lay whether these have any lands in Harwood.

REFERENCES

R1   Bolton Parish Church Registers. Bolton Central Library Archives.

R2   Records of the Manor of Manchester Court Leet from 1552 until 1846 (excluding 1687-1731) and Constables Accounts from 1612 to 1633 are on shelves in the Local Studies Unit of the Manchester Central Library.

R3   The Act for Dividing, Allotting & Inclosing the Commons & Wastes within the Towship of Harwood. Bolton Central Library Archives.
Also 'Enclosure of Harwood Commons' TLHS 1990 J J Francis.

R4   Lancashire Census Returns. 1841-1891. Bolton Central Library Archives.

R5   Statutes of the Realm. After the Magna Carta of 1215 a king's privy council of leading barons and bishops was charged with approving royal charters and statutes. Each statute was designated the venue of the 'parliament' where it was enacted and the regnal year: the first listed was Merton 20 Henry III. (1235) The Declaration of Rights of 1668 established an Act of Parliament as the overruling statute thereafter.

R6   The Great Inquest of King John 1212. The Book of Fees. PRO. Kew.
A review of landholdings and knights' service that led to Magna Carta.

R7   'Records of the Manor Court of Turton'. Transcribed by Sir Lees Knowles 1909. The Court Baron Records from 1737 to 1850 (except 1740-1745).

R8   A 'freeman' was originally a worker not tied to the manor who could leave at will. After the demise of bondage in the 1500s the term came to mean a tenant who held his land of the lord at a fixed rent and without the obligation of feudal services.

R9   Bolton Central Library Archives BN/QZ/1/118.

R10 In open-field farming, strips were ploughed communally with a furrow length (furlong) being the hauling distance between rests of an ox-team. To equalise the strips a measuring 'rod' was used and a furlong of 40 rods and strip width of 4 rods constituted a day's ploughing. This area of 160 sq rods became established as the acre. The arbitrary 'rod' varied widely and by Statute of 1340 the rod (pole or perch) was ruled to be $5\frac{1}{2}$ yds, but differing regional acres persisted well into the 1800s. The Lancashire Acre with a rod of 7 yds was common north of the Ribble and the Cheshire Acre with a rod of 8 yds was normal south of the river. Cheshire Measure is used throughout this publication.

Statute Acre	–	rod $5^1/_2$ yds –	acre $(160 \times 5^1/_2{}^2)$=	4840 sq. yds.
Lancashire Acre	–	rod 7 yds	–	acre (160×7^2) =	7840 sq. yds.
Cheshire Acre	–	rod 8 yds	–	acre (160×8^2) =	10240 sq. yds.

R11 One knight's service usually meant 'attendance with the king for forty days suitably attired for war'. Subinfeudation into smaller estates created fractions of knights' service which were generally achieved by providing service in fractions of forty days.

R12 'Lords of the Manor of Bradshaw' TLHS 1977 J J Francis.

R13 Fines and Recoveries. Two fictitious legal actions which could break an entail on a lease were in use from c1300 until abolished in 1833. They were heard at the Court of Common Pleas and recorded in Latin until 1778.
FINAL CONCORD. A purchaser (*querent*) falsely alleged that the vendor (*deforciant*) had failed to convey a property to him. The parties agreed that the freehold belonged to the querent. The Agreement was transcribed three times on a single sheet of parchment, two side by side and one across the bottom with the word *'cyrographum'* (chirograph or counterpart) written both vertically and horizontally between the copies and separated with two indented cuts. The bottom copy (*the foot of the fine*) was kept by the court and the other two copies were intended for the purchaser and vendor but as the latter did not need his, the two counterparts were usually kept together with the title deeds.
COMMON RECOVERY. Put simply, a purchaser (*demandant*) falsely claimed that he had been ejected illegally from his property by an agent of the vendor (*tenant in tail*). The demandant won the action and was awarded the freehold. The Deed of Conveyance was an exemplification of the sealed court record of the recovery.

R14 'Affetside' TLHS 1994 J J Francis.

R15 The Earldom of Derby was created by King Stephen and held by eight generations of the Ferrers family from 1137 to 1265, the five Earls and Dukes of Lancaster from 1266 until 1399 when the title merged into the crown, and nineteen generations of the Stanley family from 1485 to the present day.

R16 Commonwealth Church Survey 1650 L & C Record Society 1878.

R17 'The Ainsworth Family at Smithills Hall' 1993 John Keelan
The Friends of Smithills Hall.

R18 The Hulme Trust was formed in 1692 with an average annual revenue of
£96 which escalated to £5000 pa by the early 1800s. After a complete
reorganisation in 1881 the trust extended benefits to other schools and
colleges. They inherited a collection of 124 charters and deeds dating
from 1280 for estates in Denbigh, Middlewich, Reddish. Salford,
Manchester, Broughton, Middleton, Oldham, Bury, Kearsley, Breightmet
and Harwood. Hulme Deeds 1-124 Chetham's Library.

R19 'Harwood Hill Farms' TLHS 2004 J J Francis.

R20 'Brooke and Eskrick Families 1600-1860' Margaret Yvonne Parke IOM
Bolton Central Library Archives B929.2.BRO

R21 'Harwood Vale' TLHS 1997 J F Horridge.

R22 'Hardy Cornmill' TLHS 2001 J F Horridge.

Figure 56 *Old Green Riding Gate 1942.*
Developed during the early 1700s from a small holding. The residents at the
time were mainly employed in handloom weaving and coal mining.